THE
JAMESTOWN
FURNITURE
INDUSTRY

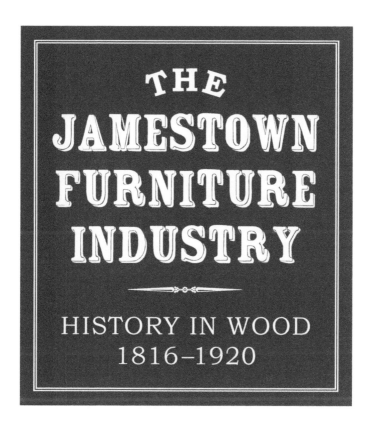

THE JAMESTOWN FURNITURE INDUSTRY

HISTORY IN WOOD
1816–1920

CLARENCE C. CARLSON

THE
History
PRESS

Published by The History Press
Charleston, SC 29403
www.historypress.net

First published 2014

Manufactured in the United States

ISBN 978.1.62619.295.9

Library of Congress CIP data applied for.

In memory of Carl A.J. Carlson, cabinetmaker and my "DAD."

Contents

Preface

The ultimate goal of this book is to compile a written history of the furniture industry in Jamestown, New York, from its inception in 1816 to the 1920s. Within the pages of this book, 112 companies are detailed and another 30-plus (because of lack of information) are given a brief history. While reading about furniture factories that employed from as few as ten to as many as four hundred skilled workers, you may ask yourself, "How did this all begin and what led to its downturn and near demise?" I will try to answer those questions.

In researching the early reasons for the development, four well-known local authors were referenced. They are considered by Jamestown historians to be authorities on the early history. In part, they wrote about furniture manufacturing being the first industry to grow out of the local lumber mills.

Elial Todd Foote, a physician and early settler, came to Jamestown in the spring of 1815 at the age of nineteen. One of his greatest accomplishments was the compiling of early newspaper articles, personal accounts, notes and letters from early pioneers tracing the growth of Jamestown. He compiled an accurate picture of Jamestown up to about the 1840s. These notes were well kept, and though some were damaged and lost, in many ways, they gave the reader an image of day-to-day life in a growing pioneer town.

Andrew Young used excerpts from the original notes and published a book in 1875, *History of Chautauqua County, N.Y.* Those original Foote documents that Andrew Young, and others to follow, used are now the property of the Prendergast Library Archives and the Chautauqua County Historical

Society. Obed Edson, a Chautauqua County historian, also wrote a book in 1894, *The History of Chautauqua County*, using some of Foote's documents. Another man who contributed much to compiling a history of the city of Jamestown was city historian Arthur W. Anderson, who published *The Conquest of Chautauqua* in 1932. His historical account of Chautauqua County and the development of Jamestown is an accurate depiction of historical locations of early Jamestown buildings. Anderson used excerpts from G.W. Hazeltine's book *The Early History of Ellicott*, published in 1885–86, and the notes by Foote. All of these books are excellent research and reading material for the person who wants to indulge in the history of Chautauqua County and Jamestown. The Jamestown City Directories, Jamestown newspapers and other booklets available for reading and research at the Fenton History Center are good sources of reference.

Many have asked me, "How did you get started on this project?" I have been a local history buff for a number of years, buying any released publication on Jamestown history and keeping my eyes open at garage and household sales for any out-of-print books. It was during the long, cold winter nights of 2001 that I began to read through a couple volumes of books in my home library: *The History of Chautauqua County and Its People*, volumes two and three, published in 1921. These books contained references to furniture factories I had never heard of before.

My dad was a cabinetmaker from Sweden who initially worked in the mines of Pennsylvania and then relocated to Jamestown to work in the furniture shops. I recognized the names of the companies where he had worked.

But there were many other companies, and in many cases, the books would tell when they were founded, the location, establishment dates and products. I formed an outline of these companies and their founders for my own research and to pass the time. By the time I was done, fifty-three furniture companies were listed, and I knew there was more to the story that needed to be investigated.

As my research continued, it became clear that the furniture industry played a major part in the development of the city of Jamestown. Unfortunately, the history books offered bits and pieces of information about the furniture companies, but an inclusive manuscript did not exist. That was all the incentive I needed, and as they say, the rest is history.

I would like to thank the Fenton History Center and its executive director, Joni Blackman, who initially supported the writing of this book by forming a book committee. The committee members include Traci Langworthy, Kathy Barber, Karen Livsey, Sam Genco and Paul Leone. Much appreciation goes to the people who have given me support (and a push when needed): Ken Prince, Norm Carlson, Kathy Foster and Dianne Carlson, just to mention a few.

Thank you to two very special friends: Pam Brown, who helped me prepare the manuscript and has been a big asset to the completion of the book, and photographer Ed Vos. Their time, support and expertise helped bring this project to fruition. My gratitude goes out to all those folks who have continued to take an interest and offer their ideas on the approach to this project.

What began as a mild interest in a bit of Jamestown's history became a work of love and respect in honor of so many of those furniture makers. They were true artisans.

Introduction

Jamestown is a city in southwestern Chautauqua County, New York. It is situated between Lake Erie to the northwest and the Allegheny National Forest to the south. It is the largest population center in the county. The city was once known as the second largest "Furniture Maker in the United States," where visitors from all over the world attended furniture expositions at the Furniture Mart Building that still stands today. Wood furniture manufacturing was a significant component of early industrial development in Jamestown. It was a direct outgrowth of the early nineteenth-century lumber industry that brought the settlers to Chautauqua County. In part, it was the reason Jamestown, this hamlet of a dozen or so families in 1815, prospered. Obed Edson wrote of Foote's account describing the hamlet of Jamestown in 1816 as little more than a ragged hole in a gloomy forest wilderness. Only about sixty acres had been cleared, and swamps, burned logs, stumps, mire holes and unpainted cabins perched on wooden blocks were the chief features of the "clearing," while surrounding this on every side a forest of majestic pines towered heavenward.

On March 6, 1827, Jamestown became a village. The population had increased from its 1815 roots to over four hundred. Men of prominence invested in the future of the village, opening a number of businesses to accommodate the growing local population. In 1827, furniture made by area shops was in its infancy. The town had one chair (Palmiter chair factory) and two cabinet shops (Breed Shop and Keyes Shop). In those early years,

Level Furniture Company. *Jamestown, New York, Historical and Industrial Review*, 1911.

Jamestown and the surrounding towns were the main source of distribution for the chairs and furniture made in these three shops.

By 1886, the population had risen to more than 5,300 residents. The village of Jamestown was made a city in March of that year. James Prendergast and most of the early founders had passed away. However, because of their insight, the temporary character of the softwood lumber industry induced other enterprises into the Jamestown industrial scene. At the top of that list was furniture. Quality-built furniture from domestic and foreign hardwood forests was the main source of income and employment.

The forests of virgin black walnut and white oak were ideal cabinet hardwoods. These hardwoods, still found today in great numbers within a one-hundred-mile radius, gave the artisan cabinetmakers a fine hardwood with a grain and beauty that was marketable in their furniture both in and out of the area.

Quartered oak and walnut from area forests were used to manufacture bedroom sets at the local companies of A.C. Norquist, Atlas Furniture and Empire. This hardwood lent itself nicely to the production of parlor and library tabletops produced at A.P. Olson Company and Maddox Table. Level

Above: Alliance Furniture Company. *Jamestown, New York, Historical and Industrial Review*, 1911.

Right: Supreme Court chair. *Courtesy of the Fenton History Center.*

Furniture and Jamestown Cabinet used cherry, another local hardwood, to make phonograph cabinets for Edison Company. Union and Alliance Furniture made some of the finest dining room furniture from the area's best Birdseye maple. Other native and tropical hardwoods for the production of office furniture produced bedsteads, bookcases and chairs.

In the 1920s, Jamestown Lounge and Jamestown Royal built upholstered chairs and lounges and were other mainstays of Jamestown's furniture industry. The United States Supreme Court purchased a number of these chairs for its judges. During World War I, the builders of torpedo boat destroyers purchased leather cushions made by Jamestown Upholstery.

This book will chronicle furniture manufacturing in Jamestown from its establishment in 1816 to the 1920s. In that period of a little over one hundred years, Jamestown rose to the status of second-largest producer of furniture in the United States.

Chapter 1

The Beginning, Breed and Keyes Shops

1816

Royal Keyes, Keyes & Breed, Wm. & J.C. Breed Co.

Date: 1816–1905
Location: Main near Fourth Street, Pine between Third and Fourth Streets, Pine and Second Streets, Willard and Winsor Streets, Jones Street and Gifford Avenue
Founders: Royal Keyes, William Breed and John Breed
Products: dining, dressing and worktables, sideboards, dressers, bureaus and stands

The Breed Company was the only big furniture manufacture supporting the growth of the town from 1823 to about the 1870s. It contributed not only by distribution and sales of its variety of furniture but also by employing many of the men who went on to become entrepreneurs in furniture. That list includes Olof and August Lindblad of Lindblad Brothers; George B. Ford of Ford, Wood & Company; Theodore Hanchett of Jamestown Lounge Company; and Samuel A. Carlson of S.A. Carlson & Son. Brothers John and Charles Eckman of Eckman Furniture had worked for the Breeds first, before purchasing the company on Jones and Gifford in 1905. The Breeds are recognized for the early development of the furniture industry in Jamestown, for their contribution to the Lakeview Cemetery Association, for the organization and growth of the

William Breed. *Courtesy of the Fenton History Center.*

First Baptist Church and other local and civic projects in the community. The Breed Company is the model for the evolution of wood furniture manufacturing in Jamestown from cottage industry to large-scale factory production. The company operated under the Breed name for more than eighty-five years, and its successors continued to produce wood furniture for nearly another half century. For its first fifty years, from the humble partnership of William Breed and pioneer Royal Keyes in 1821 through the early 1870s, the company was the single large-scale furniture manufactory in Jamestown village. The last of the Breeds' large factory facilities, built and occupied in 1892 at then 129–33 Jones and Gifford Avenue, was later purchased by the Art Metal Corporation in 1958. Art Metal became the largest metal office furniture producer in the United States.

In 1820, carpenter and joiner William Breed moved to Jamestown from Pittsburgh, where he had been employed as a cabinetmaker. Breed was born in Saratoga, New York, in 1795. His family relocated to Cayuga County, and then in 1819, William moved to Pittsburgh, where he learned his profession. In Jamestown, he met Royal Keyes, a Vermonter who had been living in the emerging logging camp for five years. Keyes was a fine mechanic and builder and the first to make furniture in Jamestown in commercial quantities. He had built a little two-story shop on the west side of Main Street in 1816, and he and journeyman cabinetmaker S.C. Colton (known as Pliney Colton) were producing some wood furniture on the first floor for the growing community. The upstairs was used by schoolteacher Abner Hazeltine during the winter of 1816–17.

Keyes was a skilled home builder. He spent much of 1821 away from Jamestown constructing a mill along the Conewango River for Nicholas Doloff. William Breed worked through the year in the furniture shop, and when Keyes returned in the fall, the two concluded a partnership agreement under the name Keyes and Breed. In early 1822, William brought his eighteen-year-old brother, John, to Jamestown from Cayuga County to join the partners. A year later, William and John Breed bought the furniture business from Royal Keyes.

Royal Keyes. *The Conquest of Chautauqua*, 1932.

The brothers continued at the location on the west side of Main Street until 1825. That year, they built their own shop on the west side of Pine between Third and Fourth Streets. They were now employing two other journeymen cabinetmakers. An article in the *Jamestown Evening Journal* from 1828 listed the variety of Breed products: dining, dressing and work tables; sideboards; dressers; bureaus; and stands. The best cherry and rock maple from the forests of Chautauqua County sold for eight to ten dollars per thousand square feet at this time. The Breeds accepted lumber or produce as

John Breed. *Courtesy of Fenton History Center.*

19

payment. It was not long before they were sending furniture on flatboats constructed for that purpose down the Chadakoin, Conewango, Allegheny and Ohio Rivers for distribution along the way.

In 1833, the company built a larger factory on the southeast corner of Pine and Third Streets. In 1895, that building housed a retail furniture store under the management of George Breed, who was also an undertaker. There may have been some manufacturing still done at the Pine Street location.

In 1895, J. Warren Fletcher wrote an article for the *Jamestown Evening Journal* reminiscing of his days as a paperboy, saying, "Fifty years ago [1845] I used to stop for a half hour or more nearly every week in the shop on Pine Street between 3rd and 4th and talk to the proprietors Wm. and J.C. Breed." Employees at that shop were Philo Morgan, William Deland, George Ford and, later, Barber Babcock and Wheaton Harrington; later still was M.W. Harrington.

After 1845, the front portion of the original shop on Pine between Third and Fourth Streets was remodeled into boardinghouses owned by Ellick Jones. Almon Partridge joined the business as partner in 1835 to handle business affairs. He died in 1837, the year a new building was completed on Willard Street east of Winsor and south of the Chadakoin in the area known as Piousville. The village's first sash and pail factories had already located in the vicinity. The Breeds purchased water power rights, and the new location was the first furniture shop in Jamestown to use water power to run planing and turning machines. Early water-powered machinery was crude and used mainly for rough cutting of wood. The finish work on the furniture was still performed by the skilled hand of the cabinetmaker. Piousville was so called because of the number of church deacons, including John Breed, who owned factories in the area. In 1839, Albert Partridge, brother to the deceased Almon, joined the firm.

In 1850, George B. Ford, who had started with the Breeds as an apprentice in 1837, was elevated to partner. William Breed's son Dewitt joined the same year. The new partnership was named Ford and Breed and located in the building in Piousville. In 1853, Dewitt bought Ford's share of the company, and the company name became the D.C. Breed Company. Dewitt Breed was born in 1826 in Jamestown to William and Clara (Jones) Breed. George Ford went on to organize his own furniture company. In 1852, Augustus Johnson, newly arrived from Sweden, became operations manager. The company continued to expand.

In 1858, Nathan and Ezra Breed, brothers of William and John, converted the tannery previously owned by Foote, Fenton and Barker near the Breeds' Willard

DeWitt Breed. *Courtesy of Fenton History Center.*

Street facility to a manufactory of agricultural implements. Judson and Dewitt Breed later acquired the site for a furniture factory powered by water and then steam. In 1862, Dewitt bought the Baker property on the corner of West First and Main Streets, and a partnership was formed with Henry Comstock and W.D. Botsford. Three years later, Botsford and Comstock left the company.

In 1866, the store of S.W. Parks and R.T. Hazzard was purchased. In 1867, Judson W. Breed, son of John, became a business partner. The firm name then changed to D.C. and J.W. Breed Company.

Distribution increased substantially with the arrival of the Atlantic and Great Western Railroad (later the Erie) to Jamestown in 1860. In 1865, the Breeds sold about $65,000 worth of furniture and had a retail store on Second Street.

By 1870, forty-five years after William and John opened their first shop, Breed Furniture became a recognized leader of family-owned furniture manufacturing in the United States. At that time, Jamestown village had a population of about 5,300. On January 1, 1870, Augustus Johnson joined the second generation of Breeds as partner. Johnson asked that his name not appear on the title.

In 1875, the company employed about fifty workmen. Generally, the Breeds were considered fair employers, which accounts for the loyalty and longevity of so many of their workers. The continued success of the company ensured steady employment. In 1875, sales increased to over $100,000, and the company was listed as wholesale agent for the Jamestown Cane Seat Company, a manufacturer of chairs.

In 1878, a further expansion added offices at 17–19 Main Street. The company showrooms at Second and Main were under the direction of John Aldrich, who was married to Dewitt's daughter Clara.

Breed
Furniture
employees.
*Courtesy of
Fenton History
Center.*

Gage Furniture Co. *Courtesy of Fenton History Center.*

In 1880, the retail store was known as Breed, Aldrich and Company. Aldrich purchased the Breed share in the retail business and then partnered with H.M. Gage at a store on Main Street under the name Aldrich and Gage.

The partners also manufactured a line of chamber suites at this location. In 1887, John Aldrich became sole proprietor of the retail outlets. He moved his business to then 100–8 Main Street, the former location of the historic Fenton Tavern. Aldrich operated at this location until 1914, when he sold out to the Field and Wright Company.

Judson Breed sold his interest in the company to his cousin Dewitt in 1879. The company name then reverted to the D.C. Breed Company. In 1881, the name again changed to the Breed Furniture Company. By now, elders William and John had retired. Dewitt was president. William died in 1883 at age eighty-eight. His brother John died in 1886 at age eighty-two. Founding brothers William and John were married to sisters Clara and Olive Jones, respectively, daughters of prominent Jamestown pioneer Solomon Jones. The Breeds are buried in Lakeview Cemetery in family plots, one for

William and his family and the other for John and his family. The Breed facility on Winsor in 1890 consisted of a five-story manufacturing structure, a brick boiler and engine house with four dry kilns and a five-story plant housing finishing rooms, warerooms, packing rooms and offices. In 1891, the company employed seventy-five workers, including six traveling salesmen. In 1892, the Breed Company moved to the new location complete with hot-air heating and electric lights at Jones and Gifford Avenue. In January 1894, with Augustus Johnson's blessing, the company incorporated under the name Breed-Johnson Furniture. Dewitt Breed died in 1896. Augustus Johnson died the

Charles Eckman. *History of Chautauqua County and Its People*, 1921.

same year. He had been partner in the Breed operation for twenty-six years. Most of his time was spent as superintendent of plant operations.

In 1896, no Breed was listed as owner of the manufacturing company. Officers of the company then were John A. Peterson, president; Oscar F. Johnson, vice-president; and Charles Eckman, secretary-treasurer. The average company wage was $1.50 per day, and the company offered an extensive line of furniture.

Water-driven machinery to make furniture used first in the Breed plant on Winsor Street was crude. Companies that followed using this machinery were ahead of the competition in some respects, but not all of the operations were done by machine. The art of fine cabinetmaking was still done by skilled cabinetmakers.

As late as 1900, the principal machines were slash saws used to cut rough lumber to length and band or circle ripsaws used to cut lumber into widths. Planers and four-sided molders were used to make the rough shape of the piece needed. A machine called a scraper was used to smooth flat surfaces after lumber had been run through the planer.

Breed Furniture. *Courtesy of Fenton History Center.*

Within the shop, a line shaft that extended inside the building was attached to an outside water wheel that ran the machinery. The individual machines received their power from a system of belts and pulleys attached to the line shaft. When you first set your eyes on the workings of these machines, you were reminded of a great large spider with long belt legs extending to the individual machine. The decorative work and finishing operations continued to be done by the hand of the skilled cabinetmaker. Later, steam was used to run the machines, and shortly after World War I, electric motors were attached directly to the machines, eliminating the need for the large belt drives.

A fire at the plant in 1904 caused major damage but no injuries. Numerous offers to relocate out of Jamestown were considered by the owners. In 1905, John and Charles Eckman purchased Breed-Johnson Furniture. The new owners elected to rebuild at the same location. While the plant was under reconstruction, the Eckmans operated from the lower floor of the Martyn Brothers building on West Fourth Street. The company continued to operate under the

John Eckman. *History of Chautauqua County and Its People*, 1921.

Breed Furniture. *Courtesy of Fenton History Center.*

Breed-Johnson name until 1912, when it became known as the Eckman Furniture Company.

By 1914, none of the Breed family was associated with furniture manufacturing in Jamestown. This was the first time in over eighty-five years that the Breed name did not appear on a listing of officers or in a company name. The link between the origins and the fabulous success of furniture manufacturing in Jamestown was broken. In 1928, the Eckmans sold their business to the Randolph Furniture Works, a division of Davis Furniture Company of Jamestown. The final listing for this company was 1955. The facility on Jones and Gifford Avenue remained empty for a year and then became part of the Art Metal Corp.

Chapter 2

Chair Manufacturing

1827

PHINEAS PALMITER JR., R.V. CUNNINGHAM CHAIR FACTORY

Date: 1827–1860
Location: East First Street, northwest corner of Third and Cherry Streets,
   Fifth and Cherry Streets, East Cherry below Third Street
Founders: Phineas Palmiter Jr. and Robert V. Cunningham
Products: flag-, cane- and wood-seat chairs

In 1827, the same year the village of Jamestown was incorporated, Phineas Palmiter Jr. opened the community's first chair factory. Although the Marshes and Harmis Willard had produced a small number of chairs in prior years, it was Palmiter who became the first tradesman to produce chairs in commercial quantities in Jamestown. His early factory was known to produce flag- and wood-seat chairs, using a combination of water-powered lathes and skilled handcrafting.

A native of Rhode Island, Palmiter was one of the first settlers to arrive in the Southern Tier. He was about twenty-four years old when he moved in 1813 to the near wilderness that was then the town of Ellicott. His father, Phineas Palmiter Sr., was a veteran of the Revolutionary War who settled on what is now Baker Street Extension. For his part, the junior Palmiter was known as a jack-of-all-trades, having experience as a millwright, carpenter, metalworker and general mechanic.

R.V. Cunningham. *The Conquest of Chautauqua,* 1932.

Phineas Palmiter. *The Conquest of Chautauqua,* 1932.

There is a cherry stand displayed at the Fenton History Center in Jamestown built in 1814 by Phineas Palmiter Jr., who gave it to James Prendergast. On March 23, 1870, the *Chautauqua Democrat* printed an article about that stand. The stand had been seen on display in one of Breed's furniture rooms and was said to be the oldest piece of furniture surviving in Jamestown, New York. Prendergast used the drawer under the top middle of the stand as a bank. No one knows how much money was placed in that drawer at any one time, but the stand remained in the Prendergast family for many years, indicating that many transactions were done before it was donated to the Prendergast Library.

Another interesting fact about Palmiter is that an early photograph of his tombstone at Lake View Cemetery was found at the Fenton History Center. It reads: "First furniture manufacture in Jamestown N.Y." This appears to be a true statement based on verification of the cherry stand. However, Royal Keyes was Jamestown's first settler to produce and sell furniture in commercial quantities part time in his shop on Main Street. In 1815, Palmiter Jr. built a twenty- by twenty-eight-foot home at the southwest corner of Main and Third Streets, not far from the home and shop of Royal Keyes.

Palmiter's chair factory opened in June 1827 on East First Street. The building was raised two stories, on the tailrace of the nearby gristmill. Situated about three hundred feet east of Main Street, the building was also very near the first woolen mill (marked today by a New York State historical marker) and not far from what became the west end of the Broadhead and Sons worsted mills. A large, long water wheel powered the two lathes and grindstone. A notice appearing in the *Jamestown Evening Journal* on June 5, 1827, advertised "all kinds of Fancy and Windsor Chairs of the newest fashion, and of the best materials and workmanship."

To help with the operation, Palmiter immediately recruited Robert V. Cunningham, a friend from Pittsburgh. Another friend, Benjamin T. Morgan, also assisted, although he stayed for only two to three years before moving to Kiantone and buying a farm.

In 1829, Cunningham actually took over the business from Palmiter. It remains unclear exactly when Cunningham bought out the founder. Whatever the date of the transfer, it seems Cunningham did not stay long in the Palmiter building. Once he had vacated, an ad was placed in the *Jamestown Evening Journal*. The following text appeared on June 30, 1830: "The building occupied by the subscriber as a chair factory with two workbenches, two water lathes, a grindstone by water, and other apparatus, suitable for chair maker

Benjamin Morgan rocker. *The Conquest of Chautauqua*, 1932.

Cunningham curly maple chair. *The Conquest of Chautauqua*, 1932.

or wheelwright. Further particulars and terms, which will be moderate, inquire of P. Palmiter Jr." Cunningham began his successful proprietorship at a new shop built in 1830 on the northwest corner of Third and Cherry Streets. In a text of the early days of Jamestown written in 1887, G.W. Hazeltine recalled, "I well remember the first power used by Cunningham. It was a foot lathe and most thoroughly was his right foot educated to the business." The remembrance attests to the fact that chair making was not an easy profession. Nor was the work particularly lucrative at this early point in Jamestown's history. Both Cunningham and Palmiter had advertised that lumber and/or produce would be received for payment of goods received. This practice was not unusual. Early settlers "paid" for many goods and services using the barter system.

Cunningham seemed devoted to the craft. About 1835, records show he operated a chair factory on Fifth and Cherry Streets, in the approximate location of the modern-day chamber of commerce building. In 1838, he added a line of cane-seat chairs to his production. The new chairs were sent downriver to sell at many of the growing towns along the way. Some years later, Cunningham erected another building on a location south of the old Sherman House (today's Covenant Manor) on Cherry Street and used it for manufacturing chairs. Cunningham and his family moved to a home at then 87 Main Street sometime after 1840.

By the mid-1800s, changes in technology signaled the end of an era in the chair industry. The business of R.V. Cunningham closed in 1860, due to heavy competition from manufacturers cranking out machine-made chairs. The mechanized factories could produce greater quantities in less time for a lower price. It was said, however, that when traders on the Ohio River could no longer obtain the Cunningham chairs, they refused to buy any other chairs.

Robert Cunningham died in 1889. At the time, he was credited with being the oldest manufacturer of furniture in Jamestown. He was preceded in death by his friend Phineas Palmiter Jr., who died in 1861 in Pittsfield, Pennsylvania, when a runaway horse threw him from a wagon. Palmiter was seventy-one years old. He is buried in Lakeview Cemetery in Jamestown.

Cunningham rush-bottom chair. *The Conquest of Chautauqua*, 1932.

JAMESTOWN, THE VILLAGE

By 1827, Jamestown had been incorporated as a village with a population of approximately four hundred inhabitants. The principal industry was still lumbering, with the village being surrounded by primeval forests of mainly majestic pines. The river system was used to export Jamestown-manufactured goods from the growing community, and the forests were slowly giving way to new buildings and streets.

At that time, there were two distilleries, one woolen factory, two wagon makers, five shoe shops and a host of other small manufactures. These small shops were sending pails, tubs, shingles, scythe snaths (the curved handle of a scythe) and rakes, among many other items, to the growing southern river towns. Other shops within Jamestown that supplied the needs of residents were hatters, blacksmiths, grocers, tanners and saddle makers. The furniture industry was also settling in Jamestown. There were two cabinetmakers, one chair factory and one sash factory.

Importing the needed supplies such as dry goods, sugar, molasses, nails, machinery for the saw and gristmills and rafting cables was no easy task. Prior to the opening of the Erie Canal in 1825, most of the goods came from the south by way of the rivers. A flatboat could have a small crew float with the current downstream to deliver the goods made in Jamestown, but it would take as many as a dozen men to bring the loaded boat of needed goods back against the current. The opening of the Erie Canal made it possible for goods to come to Jamestown by way of Lake Erie and Chautauqua Lake. This improved the importation of goods and settlers considerably.

MARSH, BELL & ROBINSON; ROGERS & BELL; FLINT & WARNER; FLINT, HALL & MOSES

Date: 1838–1855
Location: near Winsor and Willard Streets intersection
Founders: Asa Marsh, Benjamin P. Bell and Schuyler Robinson
Products: cane- and flag-seat chairs

Asa B. Marsh, Benjamin P. Bell and Schuyler Robinson were among the early chair manufacturers in Jamestown, having opened a chair shop in approximately 1838. The name of the establishment is assumed to be Marsh, Bell & Robinson because many of the early businesses were named after their proprietors. It first manufactured cane- and flag-seat chairs at a factory located near the intersection of present-day Winsor, Harrison and Willard Streets. With approximately fifteen skilled workers, the operation would have been considered medium-sized for the era.

The company changed hands multiple times through the years. Bell eventually became the sole owner, but he soon saw the need for a partner. In 1846, W.R. Rogers came into the business, and the name changed to Rogers & Bell. By that time, the company had begun to ship its chairs in a "knock-down" version to be assembled by the customer. The Rogers-Bell partnership lasted for only a short time.

In 1851, George Flint bought out Bell's financial interest in the business. Flint then formed a new partnership with his brother, Nathaniel, and Lucius B. Warner. Lucius Warner came to Jamestown in 1848 when the village had only about 2,500 inhabitants. He and Flint erected a large building near what was called the lower pond on Allen Street. According to G.W. Hazeltine, an early local historian, this building was used primarily for sawing and planing lumber. In 1854, Warner actually left the chair business and devoted his energies full time to the cutting and selling of lumber. He soon owned a planing mill on Allen Street. When this mill burned, he purchased another on Baker Street.

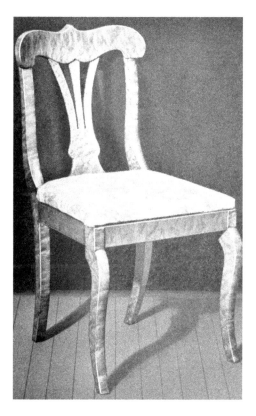

Benjamin Bell curly maple chair. *The Conquest of Chautauqua*, 1932.

With Warner's departure, George Flint brought in new partners, and the original chair business became known as Flint, Hall & Moses. This new arrangement did not last. The chair shop went out of business by 1855. As it turned out, Warner had better luck in the timber industry. By 1900, his office and lumber company were headquartered on Steele Street. He remained active in the Jamestown area until his death in 1905 at the age of eighty-two.

BENHAM & BELL

Date: 1839–?
Location: lower Main Street near First Street
Founders: Benham and Bell
Products: rocking chairs

Established in September 1839, the Benham & Bell Company produced chairs, with a specialization in Boston rocking chairs. An advertisement in the *Jamestown Journal* on September 11, 1839, noted the availability of "every variety of CHAIRS AND SETTEES, including the New and Elegant Boston Rocking Chair, all of which are warranted to be made of the best materials, and finished in a genteel and workmanlike manner." The company's small shop was located near the Breeds' 1837 factory at the "lower pond." The proprietors also owned a wareroom, a combined warehouse and show room, on Main Street. Their business may have been part of the Marsh, Bell & Robinson Chair Company.

The Boston rocking chair has a distinguished place in American furniture making history as the first mass-produced rocker. Its token design was developed in New England sometime prior to 1840. The high back and long spindles were reminiscent of eighteenth-century New England chairs, including the Windsor rocker. The Boston rocker was also known for its uniquely shaped seat, which curved down in the front and up in the rear.

There is no further information on the company.

FORD, WOOD & CO.

Date: 1850s?–1871
Location: foot of Main Street
Founders: George B. Ford and George Wood
Products: chairs and general furniture

George B. Ford was born in 1818 on the family farm. He moved to Jamestown in 1837, beginning a cabinetmaking apprenticeship at the Breed furniture factory that lasted until 1850, when he became a partner. This arrangement continued until about 1853. He also apparently partnered with George Wood in the chair-making business in the very early 1850s, as they are noted as selling a portion of their chair business to David Sampson and Robert Tyrell in 1852.

In 1869, Ezra Wood joined the business, which also operated a lumberyard while making general furniture items in a building believed to be located at the foot of Main Street. About $35,000 worth of chairs was sold in 1870, while tables were also manufactured. In 1871, Ford sold his interest in the company, which then became known as George Wood & Company. Shortly afterward, Ezra Wood also left to become a vinegar manufacturer. Ezra died on June 30, 1874, at the age of seventy-six, while Ford died on August 5, 1893, at age seventy-four.

George B. Ford. *Courtesy of Fenton History Center.*

Chapter 3

The Growth of New Factories Influenced by the Railroad Connection

1860

THE RAILROAD LINK

On August 25, 1860, the first train loaded with a few dignitaries and invited guests steamed into Jamestown on the Atlantic and Great Western Railroad line. This event celebrated the new transportation link between Jamestown and New York City and initiated a new era of growth in Jamestown's population and its industrial development. Jamestown's pioneer days had officially ended. Now workers, raw materials and finished products could be efficiently transported to meet demands. In the next few years, the increasing need for furniture created a market for the many small cabinet shops that dotted the hills of Jamestown to the north, south, east and west.

Railroad boundaries quickly expanded westward. By 1863, a rail line had been completed linking Jamestown to Meadville, Pennsylvania, and beyond to Cleveland and Cincinnati, Ohio, and even as far as St. Louis, Missouri. The railroad opened the furniture market to customers in the Midwest, as well as those in the East. The Civil War was also raging at this time, and the mass destruction of the South increased the demand for furniture, resulting in a flurry of new manufacturers. Rail links enabled Jamestown businesses to get materials for furniture production and to transport finished products to distant customers. Railroad transportation also facilitated an influx of immigrants, particularly Swedish wood artisans and craftsmen. Many of them came directly to Jamestown from the Port of New York. These skilled workers played a key role in the growth and future of Jamestown's furniture industry.

SAMPSON & TYRREL CO., SIMMONS & TYRREL CO., F. SIMMONS & CO.

Date: 1852–1868
Location: foot of Main Street
Founders: David Sampson and Robert Tyrrel
Products: chairs and general line of furniture

David Sampson and Robert Tyrrel established Sampson & Tyrrel in 1852, when they bought out the chair business of George B. Ford and George Wood located on the corner of Main and Fourth Streets. Over the years, the company also came to manufacture pieces other than chairs, under the leadership of several different proprietors. In 1854, Frank and Leander Simmons joined the small chair factory of Sampson and Tyrrel. The company then became known as the Simmons & Tyrrel Company (David Sampson sold his investment interest the following year). In 1857, the old Baptist church building was purchased, adding to their manufacturing property. On August 20, 1858, the *Jamestown Evening Journal* listed the company as a manufacturer of bedsteads and a variety of chairs.

By 1860, the firm was known as F. Simmons & Company, taking the name of an earlier established enterprise under Frank Simmons's name. The earlier Simmons Company manufactured agricultural implements. Beginning in 1860, however, that business was abandoned to begin manufacturing a general line of furniture.

The company employed approximately forty men in 1860 and was located at the time on the corner of East Second and Cross Streets. The operation was sold before the end of the decade. In 1864, Simeon W. Parks and his son-in-law, Robert T. Hazzard, purchased an interest in the company.

The following year, Alfred Tallant and Cyrus Sheldon acquired the manufacturing business. Finally, in 1866, the company's large store was sold to Comstock, Botsford & Breed. In 1868, a fire destroyed the Tallant shop. Frank Simmons, however, continued to pursue his livelihood in the furniture business. For a short time in 1875, he was the owner of John Lord and Company, a dealer in furniture and maker of lounges located at then 6–8 and 17–19 Main Street. Soon after buying the new firm, he sold it to brothers Charles E. and Willis S. Parks, who had been selling cabinet ware with five employees since 1869. The Parks brothers' business suffered a devastating blow on September 11, 1876, when fire broke out at the lower end of Main Street. The fire destroyed their shop, as well as other establishments in the vicinity. The Parks brothers never rebuilt. Meanwhile, Frank Simmons was listed in the city directory as a grocer. In 1882, he bought a lumber business.

Chapter 4

The Swedish Entrepreneurs Arrive

1869

THE SWEDISH INFLUX

Swedish immigrants were a sturdy people of high principles and strong religious beliefs. With the climate and topography of Chautauqua County similar to their country, Jamestown became a natural settlement. Many of the men were hardy, untutored lumberjacks; others had been taught the skills of the carpenter's trade; and still others were craftsmen building fine wood furniture. Finding work in those trades in the growing industrial city of Jamestown came easy. They constructed many of the early structures, literally building the city.

The influx of Swedish craftsmen that started in the late 1860s was due in part to the greatest mass migration to America by many nationalities, and the rail link offered them the transportation inland from the Port of New York. The hardy Scandinavians also settled in some of the growing towns of northeastern Pennsylvania. The opportunity afforded them in towns like Bradford, Franklin, Oil City and Titusville was due to the discovery of oil in Titusville on August 28, 1859.

One of the stories told of the Swedish movement involves Charles Ipson, a resident of Jamestown and businessman since 1866, and his part in bringing approximately fifteen new families from Titusville. In the late 1860s, there was a furniture factory located on the outskirts of Titusville, Pennsylvania. A Mr. Myers owned the shop. The business got into financial difficulties, and

Left: A.P. Olsen. *Courtesy of Fenton History Center. Right*: John Love. *Courtesy of Fenton History Center.*

in about 1869, Myers was forced to quit and close his shop. Fifteen or twenty of these skilled woodworkers, influenced mainly by Charles Ipson, came to Jamestown and went to work in the local furniture shops.

A couple of Danish cabinetmakers who came from Titusville about that time were August P. Olson and John Love. They later became the owners of A.P. Olson Company. Their company remained in business for over sixty years and served as one of the long-established employers in Jamestown during the furniture heyday.

MARTYN BROTHERS

Date: 1865–1920
Location: Fourth and Fifth Streets near Ironstone Restaurant
Founders: Marius G. Martyn and Geoffrey Martyn Jr.
Products: fine lounges, mattresses and miscellaneous furniture

Martyn Brothers, another successful furniture manufacture for over fifty-three years, was established by Marius Martyn, who purchased a parcel of property on Fourth Street from a Mr. Brown. Martyn later built the Martyn Factory, makers of fine lounges and miscellaneous furniture. The firm was known as Martyn Brothers but was solely owned by Marius.

In 1865, Marius G. and Geoffrey Martyn Jr. commenced building furniture with only two employees. At that time, the newly formed small shop produced only lounges and mattresses. The shop may have started in a building on the east side of Main Street between Third and Fourth Streets. With the growth of Jamestown in those early years, Martyn Brothers also maintained a steady growth and, by 1874, employed approximately fifty men in a shop on Fourth Street near Clinton.

By 1894, the small shop of two original employees had grown to one hundred skilled craftsmen. In 1905, a three-story, seventy-nine- by thirty-two-foot addition was added to the Fourth Street factory. The factories were in the approximate location of the former Ironstone Restaurant. In 1896, a new brick building was constructed at Fifth and Clinton. In July 1906, the West Fourth Street location was destroyed by fire. At that time, it was being leased by Golden Furniture, Art Furniture Company and M.W. Ward, a shop making interior furnishings for banks and libraries.

Martyn was out of business by 1920, but the building continued to be leased out until a fire in February 1931 destroyed the vacant building.

JOSEPH J. GATES

Date: 1867–1876
Location: lower end of Main Street (then 24 Main Street)
Founder: Joseph J. Gates
Products: cane-seat chairs

Joseph J. Gates was an early chair manufacturer in Jamestown. He established his small shop in 1867 and was one of the pioneer makers of cane-seat chairs. Beginning in 1868, Gates partnered with Thomas Langford for a brief time. By 1872, the small company had an operating capital of $500 and produced approximately one thousand chairs annually, for a gross profit of about $750. Although the exact site of the shop is unknown, it is believed to have been located at the lower end of

Main Street. In fact, Gates may have shared a building with O.G. Chase & Son, another chair manufacturer known to be located at then 24 Main Street. Wherever it was headquartered, it is clear the operation grew in the coming years.

By 1875, the business had produced approximately $4,000 worth of cane-seat chairs. But success was followed by misfortune. A fire at the lower end of West Main Street damaged the chair shop in September 1876. Gates never rebuilt the business. Records show that he died in January 1891.

SCHILDMACHER & BAUER CO.

Date: 1867–mid-1890s
Location: Chase & Son building (Main near First)
Founders: Antoine Schildmacher and Alfred Tallant
Products: kitchen furniture and chairs

Antoine Schildmacher. *Courtesy of Fenton History Center.*

Antoine Schildmacher was a furniture maker from New York City who came to Jamestown around 1865. In 1866 or 1867, Schildmacher and Alfred Tallant became partners. The partnership did not work out, and Tallant left the area. Antoine then formed a partnership with his brother-in-law, John Bauer. The business of Schildmacher & Bauer manufactured kitchen furniture and chairs. In 1870, the partnership employed thirty men. By 1872, Schildmacher's shop had an operating capital of $15,000, producing $30,000 to $40,000 worth of furniture per year. The first location was on the south side of Second Street near the present corner of Cross and Second Streets. In 1875, the city directory listed the company in the Baker Block at the southwest corner of First and West Main Streets. Another building on Main Street was listed as warerooms (warehouse and showrooms). The building near the foot of West Main Street burned in September 1876 in a large fire that consumed a number of businesses. At that time, Schildmacher employed ten men. In 1880, the company moved into a building on Steele Street and in 1884 into the factory of Chase & Son. It remained in business until the depression of the mid-1890s.

John Bauer. *Courtesy of Fenton History Center.*

O.G. CHASE & SON, CHASE & SON

Date: 1868–1896
Location: lower end of Main Street (then 24 Main Street)
Founders: Oliver G. Chase and Corbin Willard
Products: chairs

This small shop manufactured chairs at then 24 Main Street in a two-story building with a basement. The structure was just below the present-day Arcade building and the Erie Railroad tracks. In those early days, Mr. Chase would gather large quantities of rushes along the outlet to use in the seats of the chairs. Oliver G. Chase and Corbin Willard founded the business in 1868, making wood-seat chairs. Around 1870, Corbin Willard sold his share of the business to Edwin Yale. Yale's affiliation with the company was extremely short-lived. Within a year, he sold his portion to Oliver F. Chase, the son of founder Oliver G. Chase. At that time, the company's name officially became O.G. Chase & Son.

John D. Johnson. *History of Chautauqua County and Its People*, 1921.

By 1878, the Chases had an operating capital of approximately $4,000, with eighteen skilled workers producing twenty-five thousand chairs per year at a gross profit of $18,000 to $20,000. By 1883, the Main Street location operated under the shortened name of Chase & Son. When the senior Oliver Chase died in February 1887, he left his portion of the business to his son, who continued to operate the family business for years. By 1896, Chase was no longer manufacturing chairs at the Main Street address. A fire may be to blame. Fire is known to have destroyed the nearby shop of J.D. Johnson, a producer of doors, sashes and blinds. Chase went on to sell chairs at a new retail store, which was located at then 105 East Second Street. The Second Street store remained in business until approximately 1907. Oliver F. Chase died in July 1931.

LINDBLAD BROTHERS FURNITURE

Date: 1869–1915
Location: 11 Harrison Street
Founders: August and Olof Lindblad
Products: variety of furniture and veneered doors

This company was established in 1869 by a noteworthy pair of brothers from Sweden, August J. and Olof J. Lindblad. Their first location was at the foot of Main Street near the railroad tracks.

The Lindblad Company may have been the first solely owned Swedish wood furniture shop in Jamestown. August Lindblad was born in Sweden in 1838. He attended school there, learning the cabinetmaking trade. Upon completion of his apprenticeship, he decided to come to America. Arriving in 1866, he found his way to Jamestown's Swedish community. Using his cabinetmaking skills, he had no trouble finding work. One of his first jobs was working for the Breeds, the largest manufacturer of furniture in Jamestown. It did not take long for Lindblad to establish an active interest in the humane and religious progress of Jamestown. Olof Lindblad was born in Sweden in 1841. He attended school there, learning the skills of cabinetmaking. He came to the United States in 1865, moving to Jamestown by way of the Erie Railroad connection. He also had no problem finding work at the Breeds' factory, earning the princely wage of $2.50 per day.

In 1869, Olof established the Lindblad Brothers shop. At first, the shop manufactured doors, sash and blinds but soon expanded to include a line of cabinet ware. August continued in his position at Breed Furniture Company until 1868; in 1869, he joined his brother. The Lindblad Brothers shop remained in business for forty-six years and was one of the early pioneers of furniture manufacturing in Jamestown. Olof died in September 1925 at the age of eighty-four. August died on July 14, 1903.

This small factory manufactured a variety of furniture, sash, blinds and doors. After only seven years in business, on September 11, 1876, the shop burned at a loss of $3,000. Undismayed, the brothers resumed production in the rented quarters of the Warner Building near then Brooklyn Square. They remained there for about four years and then moved into the wood frame building previously known as the Weeks building, now the George B. Ford building. In May 1889, a fire broke out on the fourth floor of the Ford Building in Brooklyn Square. Lindblad Brothers and a partner, Peter Bergquist, lost only a few pieces of machinery to water damage. But a $150 mantel for A.M. Kent and one for William Broadhead, as well as patterns and material, suffered considerable damage. In that year, Lindblad Brothers built a three-story structure located at then 11 Harrison Street, and by the end of 1889, the company was specializing in veneered doors.

In 1903, tragedy struck the small business with the death of August at the age of sixty-five. In 1911, Bergquist, who had been a partner since 1889, died. The loss of these two men caused Olof to make a decision; he continued on his own until 1915, when the business was sold and Olof retired to his West Seventh Street home.

Lindblad Brothers made the curved pulpit used first at the First Lutheran Church in Jamestown. Gerhard Lang Brewing Company absorbed the location of the plant on Harrison Street in 1916.

JAMESTOWN CANE SEAT CHAIR CO.

Date: 1870–1899
Location: Taylor Street
Founder: Horace H. Gifford and R.E. Fenton
Products: chairs

The Jamestown Cane Seat Chair Company, established in 1870, was one of the most successful chair manufacturers in Jamestown. The company incorporated with two hundred stockholders. Its leadership passed into the hands of Horace H. Gifford and R.E. Fenton (only son of New York State governor Reuben Fenton) sometime after its inception. A former resident of Mayville, New York, Gifford became affiliated with multiple banking, manufacturing and real estate endeavors in Jamestown through the years. The sons of Horace Gifford were also brought into the chair manufacturing business as they came of age. While the company's specialty was cane-seat chairs, it also produced perforated-seat chairs and fancy rockers. In 1872, the company boasted approximately $50,000 in operating capital. At the helm in that year was President Orsino E. Jones, a descendant of the early pioneer Solomon Jones. Horace Gifford served as secretary and treasurer.

Also playing a leading role in the operation was the general agent for the company, Charles E. Weeks, who served as proprietor of C.E. Weeks and Company, a cabinet shop in Brooklyn Square that produced chamber sets. Of course, much of the company's success must be credited to its workforce, which included 105 employees in 1872. Women and children were hired to do piecework in their homes, weaving chair seats. Boys and girls were paid ten cents per seat, according to records, and the children typically made 6 to 10 seats per day. Together, laborers young and old produced an output of approximately 150,000 seats per year.

When the Panic of 1873 struck the nation, the Jamestown Cane Seat Chair Company was credited with offering some much-needed assistance to its workers. In the process, the company helped save Jamestown from the devastating depression. With no money to pay their large labor force, the proprietors enacted an ingenious plan to provide compensation. In place of cash wages, they issued neatly printed four-month notes to their workers. Then they purchased a grocery store, cut the prices on goods offered and accepted the notes as cash for payment of groceries the employees needed.

By 1890, the company employed approximately eighty full-time workers and a large number of outside pieceworkers. Estimates are that as many as five hundred at-home workers were weaving cane-seats for the company's chairs. Meanwhile, Horace Gifford's sons had risen to prominent positions in the company's upper echelon. In 1890, the company officers were President Frank E. Gifford, Secretary Charles H. Gifford, Treasurer William S. Gifford and Assistant Treasurer R.E. Fenton. Frank E. Gifford had an important connection to the Fenton family, as he was married to Governor Fenton's sister, Josephine. For his part, Charles H. Gifford brought experience from previous mercantile and manufacturing pursuits in Rochester, New York. He was a graduate of Fort Edward's Collegiate Institute and Russell's Military Academy in New Haven, Connecticut. He joined Frank and William in the family business after returning to Jamestown in 1880.

As the turn of the century approached, the company expanded to include distribution points for its chairs in Maine, Pennsylvania, Ohio and across New York State. As of 1893, chairs were being manufactured in a steam-powered, four-story factory at then 31–43 Taylor Street (across from the A.P. Olson Company). The building was 450 by 45 feet in size and designed in the shape of an L. As was the case with several other nineteenth-century businesses in large wooden buildings, the Jamestown Cane Seat Chair Company eventually succumbed to a devastating fire. The building on Taylor Street burned in August 1899 at a cost of about a quarter of a million dollars. The company never recovered from the disaster. Afterward, Charles and Frank Gifford went into the banking business in Jamestown. Their father, Horace H., the co-founder of the company, died in 1904 at the age of eighty-three. Charles died a decade later, in 1914, at the age of sixty-four.

WOOD & CO., WOOD & COMSTOCK

Date: 1871–1880
Location: L.B. Warner Building
Founders: George Wood
Products: miscellaneous furniture and spring beds

In 1871, the company previously known as Ford, Wood & Company became Wood & Company when George B. Ford sold out his business interest and took charge of sales for the Cane Seat Chair Company. By 1872, George Wood & Company had $27,000 in operating capital and a workforce of thirty-four to forty skilled workmen, producing $55,000 worth of furniture.

In 1874, the chair department was transferred to another local manufacture, Chase & Son. The year 1875 saw the company change its name to Wood & Comstock when Moses H. Wood succeeded George Wood and Henry J. Comstock became a partner. The company employed twenty-five skilled workmen with a working capital of $30,000. The shop at that time was located near the foot of Main Street on the west side. In the 1875 city directory, the company is listed as a manufacture of furniture and spring beds. Henry Comstock left the business in 1875 or 1876 and, with two other partners, purchased the store of Hila M. Gage located on Third Street. He produced lounges for a time until he moved to the bending works building in 1880 and sold out to A.S. Prather. A fire in September 1876 that originated in the ninety-five- by seventy-foot building of Wood and Company destroyed three other wooden buildings and caused damages to other nearby buildings. The business moved to the L.B. Warner building, but we do not know when or if another company bought it. By 1880, Wood & Company was gone. George Wood is listed in the 1879 city directory as the business manager for Barton & Company. This company was the successor to the Parks Brothers business, undertakers and embalmers. Wood died in 1890 at the age of fifty-seven. Henry Comstock died on May 5, 1883. Moses H. Wood lived in Pittsfield, Massachusetts, and no further information is known.

JAMESTOWN WOOD SEAT CHAIR CO.

Date: 1873–1892
Location: Steele Street
Founders: John J. Whitney, Seth D. Warner and Harrison C. Cheney
Products: chairs

The Jamestown Wood Seat Chair Company was another of the successful chair producers in Jamestown, remaining in business for nearly twenty years. Established in 1873 with two large buildings being constructed, John J. Whitney, Seth D. Warner and Harrison C. Cheney were the owners. The company was known for its quality line of cane- and wood-seat chairs. Until about 1876, these chairs were produced in the Prather Building on Steele Street. This building housed Prather's bending works, which produced the bent wood slats that made the arms and seats for the chairs. The building was close to the former Evans roller-skating rink on Steele Street. In 1875, the company had an operating capital of $25,000. Its fifty-five employees produced approximately one thousand chairs per week at an annual gross income of approximately $65,000. The company persevered through early misfortune and eventually came under new ownership in its second decade. In May 1876, a fire at the Prather Building on Steele Street damaged a great portion of Jamestown Wood Seat Chair's machinery and stock, as well as the bending works of Prather and the Frizzle Brothers shop. Jamestown Bedstead Company suffered water and smoke damage. Jamestown Wood Seat recovered and rebuilt in the same building. The shop may have been producing furniture in another wooden building on West First Street while the shop on Steele Street was being rebuilt. In February 1881, another fire broke out in the Prather Building, causing great damage to the Wood Seat Chair Company. The owners rebuilt once again, and with William Marsh of Jamestown, Bedstead bought the building from A.S. Prather and rebuilt its furniture shops.

In 1882, J.M. Beman occupied part of the building, producing center tables. In 1884, Whitney sold out his share of the business to Anson A. Burlin and John Cadwell. By the time he acquired his shares in the company, Burlin had established himself as a man of diverse interests and experiences. Born in Jamestown in 1842, he served in the Civil War as a young man. When he returned home, he opened a wagon and carriage factory. After running it for only one year, however, he went to Oil Creek, Pennsylvania, to try his hand in the oil business. He came back to Jamestown after his oil venture and entered the mercantile business with his brother Samuel in 1875. Their Jamestown shop at 53 Main Street offered a wide variety of items, including toys, glass, china, Parisian

John Cadwell. *Illustrated History of Jamestown*, 1900.

ware, port monies and musical merchandise. The partnership occupied Anson, off and on, for several years. For a period of time, he moved to Virginia and went into the lumber business. When he returned to Jamestown, he also found work as a pilot on a steamboat on Chautauqua Lake before finally becoming an investor in the Wood Seat Chair Company.

Once on board, Burlin and Cadwell positioned the company for expansion. By 1886, a supplementary location had been acquired on West Second Street to house offices and warerooms. In the same year, the proprietors also bought out the business started in 1873 by Edgar Paul and R.M. Johnson. That company was located on Steele Street. That location added the production of chamber sets to the company's chair-making line. The Jamestown Wood Seat Chair Company on Steele Street was out of business by 1892. Burlin died in 1907 at the age of sixty-five. John Cadwell, meanwhile, continued to manufacture bank and office furniture and may have used part of the building to do so. The Lewis H. Baker Company, which made wood packing boxes, also occupied the building. A wood frame structure on First Street that one time housed part or all of Jamestown Wood Seat burned in June 1897. At that time, L.G. Cowing was producing some chairs on the site. The fire also destroyed houses located on the West Terrace of First Street.

JAMESTOWN BEDSTEAD CO.

Date: 1873–1904
Location: Steele Street (near skating rink)
Founders: William A. Marsh and Rufus P. Shearman
Products: bedsteads, tables and cribs

Established first by William A. Marsh and Rufus P. Shearman under the company name of Shearman and Marsh in 1873, the name soon changed to Jamestown Bedstead Company. From this beginning, one of the most successful companies in Jamestown furniture history was born. The company was located in the Prather Building, a mammoth brick structure on Steele Street above the Warner Dam. The building was built by A.S. Prather, whose occupation included the selling of furniture, upholstered goods and feathers. He was also an undertaker. From the outset, Jamestown Bedstead produced mainly wooden bedsteads (framework for supporting the springs and mattress) and cribs.

William Marsh was born in 1840 in Belmont, Massachusetts. He attended public school there and worked on his father's farm; later, he held a position as a clerk in Boston. He came to Jamestown in 1873, and soon after his arrival, he became one of the founders of Jamestown Bedstead Company.

In 1874, the operating capital was approximately $20,000, with thirty-five to forty employees and $50,000 in sales. A fire broke out in the Prather Building in May 1876. Even though no fire damage occurred, there was considerable smoke and water damage. The shop was rebuilt in the same

William A. Marsh. *Illustrated History of Jamestown,* 1900.

building. Shearman retired in 1878, and in 1880, he and his brother went into partnership, establishing Shearman Brothers, another successful furniture factory in Jamestown located near the Prather Building. Shortly after Shearman's retirement, the name changed to Jamestown Bedstead Works.

In 1881, the Prather Building was sold to William Marsh and the owners of Jamestown Wood Seat Chair Company after another fire damaged the brick building. These two companies rebuilt their shops in the same building and continued in business.

In 1890, the company expanded by increasing the size of the plant to accommodate an additional increase in volume. The brick building was now four stories in size, 120 by 50 feet in dimension and operated on steam power. Besides the main building, the firm also operated a dry kiln, 75 by 25 feet in dimension, and an engine and boiler house, 40 by 30 feet. Finally, elegantly appointed 40- by 20-foot offices were added. In that year, Daniel H. Post, Alzenis W. Crum and Charles Ipson joined Mr. Marsh, and the concern changed its title to Jamestown Bedstead Company.

Charles Ipson was born in August 1846 in Bornholm, Denmark, the same town A.P. Olson and John Love came from. He was the son of Hendrik Ipson, who was the discoverer of Portland cement. Portland cement was used in the underwater construction of bridges and revolutionized that industry. Charles left Bornholm in 1866 and at the age of twenty was already a skilled cabinetmaker. He first settled in Warren, Pennsylvania, and went right to work as a cabinetmaker. In that same year, he moved from Warren and relocated in Jamestown. He followed his trade as a cabinetmaker by working at a number of plants for about six years. After that period, he went to work for Jamestown Bedstead, a leading crib and bedstead manufacturer. The company was sold to Henry Robertson in 1905, and Ipson was promoted to vice-president of this new company, H.P. Robertson Company.

Charles Ipson was identified as an important resident of Jamestown by becoming interested in proper city government and sanitary hygienic environments. He was a member of the Jamestown Board of Health for many years and was responsible for adopting the disposal of garbage laws used in the city for many years, some of which are still on the books. Ipson was concerned that young men and women working in the factories did not have opportunities to complete their formal education. He established a night school system, conducting classes in his home for many years. Charles Ipson died in 1926 at the age of eighty.

In 1898, the company further expanded its product line to include the manufacture of tables. In 1900, William Marsh was financial manager, Charles Ipson was general superintendent and Alzenis W. Crum and Harry P. Robertson were their principal sales representatives. In that year, the output of the plant was about half beds and half tables. Its specialty was a cheap bed and crib and a medium-priced table. The company employed approximately sixty men. The last listing for Jamestown Bedstead Company was 1904. In 1905, it became part of H.P. Robertson Company.

A.P. OLSON CO.

Date: 1874–1903
Location: Taylor Street
Founder: A.P. Olson
Products: tables, hall trees and tabourets

This company was built entirely on the character and hard work of its founder, August P. Olson, and his partner, John Love. They were totally dedicated to the company throughout their entire business lives. This dedication to quality workmanship was why A.P. Olson Company endured for over sixty years.

August Olson was born in 1849 in Bornholm, Denmark. He was educated in the Danish school system and learned the cabinetmaker's trade. He worked at his trade in Denmark until he was nineteen years old. In 1868, he came to America and settled in Titusville, Pennsylvania. As a skilled cabinetmaker, he quickly found work in a local shop. He relocated to Jamestown in 1874 after his employer in Titusville closed the business. He established a small table shop under the name of A.P. Olson Company in the old George Wood Building that burned in 1876. Olson then moved his shop to the Warner Building on West Main Street near the Erie Railroad tracks. As the small cabinet shop grew, Olson's need for a partner became evident. In 1878, a cabinetmaker named John Love, who possessed a good mechanical and business ability, became a partner in the Olson shop. These men would become very successful businessmen and instant friends.

John Love was born in Denmark on December 5, 1848. He obtained a good education in Denmark and learned the trade of a cabinetmaker. In 1868, at the age of twenty, he arrived in the United States. He settled in Titusville and quickly found work as a cabinetmaker. He may have met Olson at that time, but no reference to that acquaintance is noted. In 1872, Love came to Jamestown as a journeyman cabinetmaker for George Martin and others in the Jamestown area. By 1878, Love had become a partner with August Olson in the A.P. Olson Company. A friendship developed between the men that would last until the death of Olson in 1919 at the age of seventy. John Love died in January 1923 at the age of seventy-five.

In 1886, a fire forced them to move to then 18–24 Steele Street. By 1887, a new ironclad 55- by 180-foot building of four stories located on Taylor Street became the new address for the growing table shop. Additions to the building were made, and by 1892, a forty-horsepower engine ran the machines. In 1900, the company employed about thirty-five craftsmen. They produced a high-quality parlor and library table, pedestals, hall trees and tabourets (a low stand or stool) in about seventy-five patterns made of quartered oak and mahogany. The tops of the tables were Italian and Knoxville marble and polished quartered oak. A.P. Olson had a large and very select trade, with sales covering the central, middle and New England states.

Through the long business careers of Olson and Love, they maintained most cordial and satisfactory relationships with their employees. Olson Company was the first exclusive finely crafted table maker in Jamestown with a company slogan of "Best Material and Workmanship." The company name was changed in 1902–3 to the Diamond Furniture Company, and the sons of Olson and Love joined the business. However, the senior Olson and Love still owned the company and for years after took an active part in the production of their quality furniture.

GEORGE B. FORD CO.

Date: 1875–1883
Location: Brooklyn Square and Forest Avenue
Founders: George B. Ford
Products: tables

George B. Ford established this company in 1875 to manufacture tables. Its first location was at the foot of Main Street. Ford was born in 1818. His early years were spent on his father's farm helping with chores and learning the ways of pioneer life. In 1837, at the age of eighteen, he left the farm and relocated to Jamestown. In that year, Ford found employment as an apprentice for the Breed Furniture Company, learning the cabinetmaking trade. In 1850, the hard work paid off, as he was offered a partnership in the Breed business. He would remain in that position until 1853. He was one of the investing partners in a small furniture shop with George and Ezra Wood. In 1871, Ford left that business and until about 1873 was in charge of sales at the Cane Seat Chair Company before establishing the George B. Ford Company. In 1876, the business suffered damages when a fire broke out in the Wood and Company Building on Main Street near the railroad tracks and the race on West First Street. Ford soon found another building in Brooklyn Square, the old C.E. Weeks frame building at the south end of the square.

In 1883, George M. Hodgkins was brought into the business. The company became known as Ford & Hodgkins Co. Just five years later, in 1888, Ford retired from the business. He died in August 1893 at the age of seventy-four. Another furniture man, John Cadwell, succeeded him. Cadwell had previously been one of the owners of Jamestown Wood Seat

Chair Company. In 1889, the Weeks Building burned, and by that time Ford owned the building. Hodgkins and Cadwell suffered a great loss and moved into the new brick building adjoining and extending along Forest Avenue.

J.R. NEWMAN

Date: 1875–1889
Location: C.W. Weeks Building
Founders: Jared R. Newman
Products: beds and lounges

Jared R. Newman was born in 1832. Shortly after arriving in Jamestown from Franklin, Pennsylvania, he started in the furniture business. He founded this small shop in 1876 with four employees. In 1881, they moved to a larger building and employed thirty to thirty-five skilled workmen. Jared died in 1887, and his son Harry J. took over the business, changing the name to H.J. Newman and Company in 1889. In that year, the Weeks Building (owned by George Ford) housing the Newman business burned.

SPLINT SEAT CHAIR CO., MARSH & FIRMAN

Date: 1877–1888
Location: then 42 Winsor Street (near Jamestown Lounge)
Founders: Daniel A. Marsh and Benjamin F. Firman
Products: chairs

The Splint Seat Chair Company was established in 1877 by Daniel A. Marsh and Benjamin F. Firman. In 1881, the company was known as Marsh & Firman, makers of splint-seat, double cane–seat and carpet chairs. It was located in the Prather Building. In February 1881, it suffered great loss in a fire. In 1882, the operation moved into a new factory located at then 42 Winsor Street, near the Jamestown Lounge Company. The three-story building was approximately forty by one hundred feet in size. The last listing was in the 1888 city directory.

PERFORATED CHAIR SEAT CO.

Date: 1878–1888?
Location: then 40 Winsor Street
Founder: Henry C. Hitchcock
Products: chairs

Henry C. Hitchcock established this chair manufacturing business around 1878. The company added cane-seat chairs to its line in 1884. At that time, it was located at then 40 Winsor Street. In 1887, the company was sold to Lewis Hall. No further information appears about the company after that year. The 1888 Jamestown City Directory identifies Jamestown Lounge as the occupant of the Winsor Street location.

S.A. CARLSON & SON

Date: 1878–1898
Location: then 6–10 Willard Street
Founders: John F. Carlson and Samuel S. Carlson
Products: chamber sets

Founders John F. Carlson and Samuel S. Carlson established this small shop in 1878. They were formally known as the S.S. Carlson Company, established about 1870. The company made chamber sets and in its established year had three employees in a plant at then 6–10 Willard Street. In 1889, the plant was a three-story building forty by seventy-five feet in dimension. Steam and water powered the latest woodworking machinery. It employed approximately fourteen workmen and produced one thousand cheaper-grade chamber sets per year. In 1890, Samuel S. Carlson sold out to Samuel A. and Charles L. Carlson. Samuel A. Carlson left the day-to-day managing of the business around 1895. He bought an interest in a bilingual weekly newspaper read by the Swedish families moving into Jamestown. His interest in politics would lead him to become one of the most important and loved mayors in the city of Jamestown. He was responsible for much of the industrial growth and modernization of the city in the early and mid-twentieth century.

In 1892, Charles sold out to Oscar W. Erickson and John A. Burch. Soon after, the name changed to S.A. Carlson & Company. In 1894, the shop employed about twenty workers with an annual gross business of $20,000. The S.A. Carlson Company was gone by 1898, and in 1899, Jamestown Bedspring Company is listed in that location on Willard Street.

THE GROWING FURNITURE INDUSTRY

During the 1870s, more workers were employed in the furniture industry than in any other industry in Jamestown. This trend would not last long, as the woolen industry had been established and new plants were being built employing larger workforces.

Most of the furniture at that time was produced by the skilled hand of the cabinetmaker without the costly use of machines. This kept the investments small, with many a shop owner working next to his employees. They produced furniture with a greater margin of sales profit. However, as the years progressed, they could not produce a greater quantity like the large factories with new machine technology established much later. After 1860, the expanding need for furniture created a market for many of these small cabinet shops. They dotted the hills of Jamestown in all directions. The established railroad link opened the door to the midwestern states' need for furniture.

LANDON & CO.

Date: 1878–1886
Location: foot of Main Street
Founder: August J. Landon
Products: beds, headboards, miscellaneous furniture

This company was established around 1878 by August J. Landon. It was a small company that manufactured beds, headboards and miscellaneous furniture. In 1886, after only nine years, Joseph M. and William L. Himebaugh succeeded Landon. The Himebaugh shop was located at then 2 Main Street. The company later became Himebaugh Bros. and moved to a new location.

SHEARMAN BROTHERS CO.

Date: 1879–1962
Location: Shearman Place (Brooklyn Square)
Founders: Rufus P. Shearman and L.H. Larkin
Products: lounges, couches and sofa beds

Colonel Silas Shearman, the father of Addison and Rufus, was an early settler in Jamestown and by trade a saddle and harness maker who opened a harness shop in 1827. Rufus went to work for his father in 1854. The younger brother, Addison, would follow in about 1865. Silas retired in 1870, and the brothers ran the harness business. Before long, they were involved in various other businesses in the Jamestown area. This lasted until about 1881, when the brothers founded the upholstery shop.

Rufus Shearman, born in Jamestown in 1831, was educated at the Jamestown Academy and went to work for his father in the harness shop upon completion of his education. Rufus died in September 1894 at the age of sixty-three.

Shearman Brothers. *Illustrated History of Jamestown*, 1900.

Shearman Brothers logo. *Courtesy of Fenton History Center.*

Addison Shearman was born in Jamestown in 1843, the younger of the brothers. He was educated at the Jamestown Academy and entered the Jamestown office of A. & G.W.R.R., where he learned the trade of telegraph operator. In August 1862, Addison enlisted in the Union army (112th New York Volunteers). He returned to Jamestown after the Civil War and went to work for his father and brother in the harness shop. In 1881, Addison became a partner in the newly formed company.

Frank E. Shearman was born in Jamestown in 1857, the son of Rufus, one of the founders of Shearman Brothers. Frank was educated in the Jamestown public schools and after graduation went to work at Jamestown Bedstead Works as a shipping clerk. He remained there from 1874 to 1877. He then spent thirteen years in the Bradford, Pennsylvania oil district. In 1890, Shearman was associated with Shearman Brothers as a shipping clerk. Hard work and perseverance paid off, and in 1892, he became a partner in the business. In 1902, he became president of the company.

During a brief period in 1879, this small upholstery shop was known as R.P. Shearman and L.H. Larkin. Addison Shearman bought out Larkin in

1880 and, with his brother Rufus, established Shearman Brothers in 1880. Their first location was on East Second Street. By 1882, the success of the business allowed them to move into a larger building. The new shop was a large four-story ironclad building at then 25–41 Shearman Place, close to the now Warner Dam. The company specialty was lounges, couches and sofa beds, and for over eighty years, it produced furniture at that location.

In October 1883, the factory on Shearman Place burned. A five-story structure was built at the same location, with 26,400 square feet of floor space, along with an engine house, dry kilns and lumber storage houses.

By 1891, the company had grown to include six salesmen on the road at all times, with an extensive wholesale trade throughout New York and adjoining states. Portions of New England, the Middle Atlantic, southern and western states were also included.

In 1896, due to astonishing growth, Shearman Brothers employed approximately eighty to one hundred men at an average wage of ten dollars per week and was one of the largest furniture employers in Jamestown. Its annual sales were about eighteen thousand lounges. The company was incorporated in 1901 and the name changed to Shearman Brothers Company. The operating officers of the company were Frank E. Shearman and Fred J. Shearman, father and uncle of the founders. In 1902, the president and treasurer was Frank Shearman; the vice-president was Eugene S. Hemmenway; and Edward L. Derry was secretary.

Shearman Brothers. *Courtesy of Fenton History Center.*

Jamestown Panel & Veneer. *Jamestown, New York, Historical and Industrial Review*, 1911.

A description of the comfort of their lounges can be found in the 1900 *Illustrated History of Jamestown* by editor Verrnelle A. Hatch. It reads, "You can rest anywhere on a Shearman lounge and your spine will be, not only safe from stealthy assault, but it will be soothed, comforted and put at peace with all the world."

Shearman's success continued, and it bought out the interest of William Maddox at Maddox Table Company in 1919, becoming the largest furniture employer in Jamestown.

The Shearman Brothers Company was bankrupt by 1963. In 1965, a large fire destroyed a portion of the old manufacturing plant. In 1967, Jamestown Veneer and Plywood (plant 3) occupied the location of the remaining building.

Y.W. BURTCH & CO.

Date: 1880–1906?
Location: then 20 Winsor Street
Founder: Yale W. Burtch
Products: chairs

Yale W. Burtch established this chair manufacturing shop in 1880 at 20 Winsor Street. In 1889, Lewis Hall came into the business as the young man's partner. A native of the town of Carroll, Hall was a well-educated older man whose schooling had led him toward a career in law. Beginning in 1847, however, he turned his interests toward business and manufacturing. At the time Hall joined Burtch's company, he was the proprietor of the Perforated Chair Seat Company located next to the Burtch Building. In fact, Burtch may have bought out or merged his interests with the Perforated Chair Seat Company around the time of his partnership with Hall. There is no record of Perforated Chair Seat after 1887. Y.W. Burtch & Company's Winsor Street location boasted a four-story factory building about 125 by 40 feet in size. A fifty-horsepower steam engine powered the operations. The building was also equipped with the latest woodworking devices necessary for the expeditious production of fine furniture. In addition to fine rockers and dining chairs, the company made a variety of cane-seat, double-seat and perforated-seat chairs. Most products were shipped to the tri-state (New York, Pennsylvania and Ohio) area. By 1896, the company employed forty to fifty men at an average wage of $1.50 per day.

The company continued to operate well into the twentieth century, although under entirely different ownership. The business became Jamestown Chair around 1906. By that time, Lewis Hall had passed away. He died in 1902 at the age of eighty-seven. Yale Burtch lived for several more years. He died in 1927 at the age of sixty-seven.

A.C. NORQUIST CO.

Date: 1881–1965
Location: then 415–21 Chandler Street
Founders: August C. Norquist and Charles J. Norquist
Products: bedroom furniture

Both August and Charles Norquist were born in Sweden and were brought up working on the family farm in Smoland. August was born in 1857 and came to the United States in 1869 with his mother, sister and brothers. August was only twelve years of age when he arrived in the United States and had very little formal education. He worked with his father building houses in Jamestown and on the family farm. Times were hard, and money was always in short supply. August left the family farm to work for a farmer in Levant for ten dollars a month. He returned to Jamestown again looking for a better job. He was one of the first twelve employees to learn how to cane at Jamestown Seat and Chair Company. After leaving Jamestown Seat and Chair, he did some hand woodcarving and took up the cabinetmaker's trade for Martyn Brothers located on Fourth Street. In 1880, August left for Chicago, hoping to earn more money, but returned to Jamestown in February 1881. August and Charles then started a small cabinet shop in the barn of their father's farm. August C. Norquist died in 1926 at the age of sixty-nine, after a long career in furniture manufacturing.

Charles was born in 1850 in Sweden, and in 1869, he left for America by himself. His first job was as a wagon maker. He next went into cabinetmaking, learning to make roll-top and secretary desks. By 1881, the skills learned in cabinetmaking were sufficient for Charles and his younger brother to set out on their own business venture. The Norquist Furniture Company would go on to become one of the largest manufactures of fine bedroom furniture in the United States. This company would bear the distinction of being one of the pioneers responsible for the ranking of Jamestown as the second-largest furniture manufacturing center in the United States. This distinction was achieved largely due to the superior quality of its product, both in materials and workmanship. The company had such pride in its workmanship that its policy was no article of furniture was shipped from the factory unless it passed a set of rigid inspection requirements.

The Norquist brothers founded their company in 1881 and began by building handmade bedroom furniture in their father's barn. The starting capital consisted of $130, plus a Colt revolver that sold for $65 and a stove furnished by Charles that brought $32. To make the first articles of furniture, the brothers borrowed a circular saw and a few simple tools. They worked twelve to fourteen hours per day building furniture. The first six bedroom sets sold for $14 each. After six months in business, the profit from the sale of their bedroom furniture was paying rent and expenses, with the partners earning only $0.25 each per day. The next six months were better. They earned $1.25 to $1.30 each per day. The increase in production forced them to move from the farm to a building at 700 East Second Street. Frank Stranburg was brought in as a partner in 1882. He stayed only one year, becoming one of the founders of Atlas Furniture Company in 1883.

A near-fatal bout with typhoid fever lasting four months forced August out of the day-to-day business. This was a dismal time for him. Finally, in 1882–

Norquist brothers. *History of Chautauqua County and Its People*, 1921.

83, the brothers' hard work paid off. Dun & Bradstreet credit directory listed them with a worth of $1,500 and a medium credit rating.

Charles sold out in 1883 and started his own business manufacturing roll-top desks in a building on Chandler Street under the name of Charles J. Norquist Company. In 1888, the C.J. Norquist Company was located in the Ford Building, previously C.W. Weeks building. In May 1889, a fire broke out on the fourth floor of the Ford Building. Norquist sustained a heavy loss, with several completed and in-process desks being destroyed.

In 1883, Andrew P. Nord (a Norquist brother)* joined the business. His trade was that of a tailor working in Jamestown. He gave up that trade to join his brother as a partner in the furniture shop. In 1889, another brother, Frank O. Norquist, joined the business. In 1896, this company that began in a barn employed seventy-five to eighty men at an average wage of $1.50 per day. The company was doing about $75,000 of business a year.

---

*. Nord was the family name in Sweden. The name was changed on the request of their minister in Sweden; Andrew did not make the change. The name *Nord* being the derivative, the termination *quist* simply means "branch of."

A.C. Norquist & Co. (wooden building). *Illustrated History of Jamestown*, 1900.

Andrew P. Nord was born in Sweden on May 1, 1854. He was the second of four brothers. He was educated in the home schools in Sweden and had some knowledge of the trade of a tailor. He came to the United States in 1869 with his family, settling in Jamestown. His first job was that of a journeyman tailor in the establishment of William H. Proudfit located at 206 Main Street. Andrew was intensely religious and strongly inclined to a life in the ministry at an early age. He left the Proudfit store for Chicago to pursue a course in theological study in the Swedish Methodist Episcopal Church. He finished the course but chose to come back to Jamestown and work again in the Proudfit store until he joined his brothers at the A.C. Norquist factory in 1883.

In 1900, the company built a four-story wood frame structure fifty by ninety feet in size on Chandler Street. The former location at East Second Street was sold and occupied by Jamestown Cabinet Company. In July 1903, plans were underway to house new machinery for veneer manufacturing. The machines would be housed in a new twenty-four- by fifty-foot two-story frame building near the main building. This manufacturing would all but eliminate the need for outside buying of veneered wood.

Jamestown Cabinet Company. *Jamestown, New York, Historical and Industrial Review*, 1911.

Union Furniture Co. *Jamestown, New York, Historical and Industrial Review*, 1911.

Norquist fire. *Courtesy of Fenton History Center.*

The Norquist building located at then 415–21 Chandler Street burned on May 6, 1904, suffering a $50,000 loss to the business and, much worse, the death of Andrew Nord. He was overcome by smoke searching for trapped workers in the burning building. During the rebuilding of a new factory, a sample line was produced and sales began to roll in. Century and Union Furniture, two local companies owned by the Nord family (who were also cousins of the Norquists), supplied the resources needed to build the pieces.

After suffering two fires that almost wiped it out financially, the company completed its rebuilding process in just four months and a week. The new building fronted on Chandler Street Extension. The building was made of brick and was as nearly fireproof as technology at the time could make it. The structure was four stories high, and adjoining the rear of the factory was an engine room 30 by 40 feet in size. The dry kiln was 80 by 90 feet with storage capacity of 100,000 feet of lumber. The kiln building was separate from the main building in case a fire broke out. In the rear of the new factory building, away from the main structure on the site of the old building, was a lumberyard. The Erie Railroad extended a switch to the new factory, which provided better rail connections for shipping and receiving of raw material and finished goods.

Norquist Allied Furniture. *History of Chautauqua County and Its People*, 1921.

The new plant was completed in September 1904, and the production of its specialty, high-quality bedroom furniture resumed. In November of that year, the A.C. Norquist Company incorporated with August as president and Frank Norquist as secretary and treasurer.

In 1910, a new building was added, housing an office, shipping department and stockroom. By 1911, the Norquist Company employed 125 skilled workers in various departments. It was one of Jamestown's largest furniture manufacturers. In 1918, Frank sold his interest, using the money to establish Allied Furniture.

By 1920, the company's major product line was still fine bedroom furniture. Dinettes and occasional pieces would be added in future years. Domestic and tropical hardwoods such as mahogany, Circassia walnut, oak and Birdseye maple were used to produce the furniture. The furniture made at the Norquist plant not only sold in the United States but also extended to British Columbia. The company had a full-time eighteen-man sales force. The Norquists were great innovators. Eliminating the need for outside buying, they built much of the hardware used on their furniture. One example was the folding table leg mechanism used on their card tables.

Norquist was a well-known name in Jamestown furniture manufacturing for over eighty years. Its location on Chandler Street across the street from Marlin Rockwell Corporation (MRC) is now a parking lot for Weber Knapp. The Norquists sold out to an outside group in 1965, and another link to the past was gone.

SWEDISH FURNITURE CO.

Date: 1883–1887
Location: East Second Street
Founders: Lawrence E. Erickson and Gustave Holmberg
Products: bedroom furniture

The Swedish Furniture Company was established in 1883 by Lawrence E. Erickson and Gustave Holmberg. Holmberg was listed as president and Erickson as secretary and treasurer. Holmberg was born in Sweden in August 1848. He came to the United States in 1869 and made his way to Frewsburg, New York, where he made his home on East Oak Hill Road. He moved to Jamestown for seven years but later returned to his Frewsburg home. Erickson was born in Sweden in 1855. He came to Jamestown when he was twenty-four years old. He died at the age of fifty in August 1905.

The first plant was located on East Second Street and manufactured bedroom furniture. In 1883, five board members were added. Two of

Charles A. Johnson. History of Chautauqua County and Its People, 1921.

those members were Frank O. Strandberg and Charles A. Johnson. Strandberg had previously been with the Norquist Company. These additional board members provided the company with a larger operating capital.

In 1885, a fire destroyed the plant. It relocated to the old Academy building located at then 301 Harrison Street. In 1887, the company moved to a plant in Randolph, New York. Fifteen new stockholders were added to the group of investors. In that same year, the company began operating under the new name of Atlas Furniture Company. The operating body of the company would continue to stay about the same as with the Swedish Furniture Company. Atlas moved back to Jamestown in 1889.

PHILLIPS, MADDOX & CO.

Date: 1886–1886
Location: then 22 Steele Street
Founders: William Maddox, Hurley L. Phillips, Charles W. Morgan and Lynn F. Cornell
Products: tables

This small furniture shop first operated under the name of Beman, Breed & Phillips. It produced a parlor table made of black walnut with French walnut burl veneers and a marble top. William Maddox moved to Jamestown from Scranton, Pennsylvania, in 1885. He operated a small business at then 10 Washington Street under the company name of Maddox Reclining Chair Company. He purchased an interest investment in the company.

Maddox reclining chair. *Courtesy of Fenton History Center.*

In 1886, Maddox bought out the business interest of J.M. Beman and Charles A. Breed, changing the company name to Phillips, Maddox & Company. The small furniture shop was located at then 22 Steele Street. In a little over a year, Hurley L. Phillips became one of the founders of Jamestown Lounge Company, selling out his investment in Phillips, Maddox to Charles W. Morgan, and the name changed to Morgan, Maddox & Company.

William Maddox. *History of Chautauqua County and Its People,* 1921.

HIMEBAUGH BROS.

Date: 1886–1928
Location: then 14 Steele Street
Founders: Joseph, William, George and Lyle Himebaugh
Products: spring beds, cots and cribs

Joseph, William, George and Lyle Himebaugh established the former Landon & Company furniture factory as Himebaugh Brothers in 1886. The company first manufactured spring beds, cots and cribs in a location at then 14 Steele Street. The product line was later expanded to include the manufacture of dining room furniture. By 1889, the company was in a three-story building at 201–3 Harrison Street. The structure was forty by ninety feet and used steam power. In 1890, the company employed fifteen to twenty men. It was considered a medium-sized Jamestown furniture shop. In 1906, the company suffered the loss of its building to fire. In 1907, it relocated to a building on Hallock Street. The company enjoyed continued growth at that location, and in 1913, it bought a four-spindle automatic carver. In 1927, the company was sold to Davis Furniture. The building later became part of Automatic Voting Machine (AVM) and still exists.

William L. Himebaugh was born in 1854. He had been a farmer and worked in sawmills and the oil region of Pennsylvania. He died in 1930.

MORGAN, MADDOX & CO.

Date: 1886–1891
Location: then 560 East Second Street
Founders: William Maddox and Charles W. Morgan
Products: tables

This furniture shop was established in 1886 by William Maddox and Charles W. Morgan. It also made the Maddox reclining rocking chair at a location on 10 Washington Street. This shop made parlor and library tables. In 1888, the company was located at then 560 East Second Street (at the corner of present-day Second and Cross Streets). In that year, the officers of the company were Charles W. Morgan, William Maddox and Clayton E. Bailey.

Charles W. Morgan was born in Randolph in 1855. He was educated in the common school system in Randolph. Morgan went on with his education at Chamberlain Institute, graduating at the age of sixteen. Morgan's first job was as a bookkeeper and clerk at a grocery store in Randolph, New York. He stayed there until February 1874, when he went to Kansas, continuing in the grocery business. However, this lasted less than a year. Morgan returned to Randolph and found a position as a clerk and bookkeeper at a hardware store. In 1881, Morgan moved to Jamestown and purchased a plumbing and heating business located on the corner of Third and Spring Streets. In 1885, he was forced to leave the business because of health reasons due to inhaling lead fumes while plumbing pipes.

Clayton Bailey. *Illustrated History of Jamestown*, 1900.

In 1886, after almost a year of recuperation, he organized Maddox Chair Company with William Maddox, the inventor of the reclining rocking chair. After less than a year, the company became Morgan, Maddox & Company. In 1890, Morgan sold his interest in the company to the Bailey family.

Clayton E. Bailey was born in Jamestown in 1865. He was educated in the Jamestown public school system. Upon graduation, he worked for three years as a clerk in the Chautauqua County Bank of Jamestown. In 1886, he entered the firm of Morgan, Maddox & Company. Clayton Bailey moved on and became president of Art Metal Corporation in 1913 or 1914. Art Metal was formerly known as Fenton Metallic Company. He died in 1918 at the young age of fifty-four.

In 1890, the two-story 120- by 60-foot Second Street location housed the finishing department and warehouse. The manufacturing was done in a four-story 150- by 60-foot building located at then 22 Steele Street. In the Steele Street location, the woodworking machines were all run by steam power, a relatively new way to cut and plane wood. In that year, the company employed ninety to one hundred skilled workmen who built parlor and library tables. The specialty of the house was the production of a high-grade table of wood with plush marble tops. After 1891, the company became Maddox & Bailey. Morgan became one of the founders of Morgan Manufacturing Company located at 3–7 Ashville Avenue (Fairmount Avenue). The Steele Street location was occupied by another furniture manufacturer, Benson, Hand & Frisbee.

THE FURNITURE BOARD OF TRADE

In 1886, the Jamestown Furniture Board of Trade was organized. It was established to give mutual aid and assistance to furniture shops. Attention was given to strikes and unjust demands made on the members of the association by employees or labor organizations. The board endeavored to settle all difficulties using proper arbitration.

C.E. WEEKS & CO.

Date: 1886?–1894
Location: south end of Brooklyn Square
Founder: Charles E. Weeks, Corban Willard and Frank Davis
Products: chamber sets and extension tables
The C.E. Weeks Company was established in about 1886. The three original founders were Charles E. Weeks, Corban Willard and Frank Davis. A labor force of twenty-five produced chamber sets and extension tables in a portion of a large, four-story wood frame building at the south end of then Brooklyn Square, a place later called the Ford Block. Part of the original thirty-five- by eighty-foot building had been a woolen factory. It was built in 1848 and used as such until 1865 by owners A.F. Allen and Daniel H. Grandin. W.J. Weeks purchased the structure in 1865, built an addition to the east end of twenty by sixty feet and added a fourth story to the original building. In 1886, C.E. Weeks bought out the other investors and became sole proprietor of the business. It is uncertain if he was still producing furniture or was only operating a furniture store located on the fourth floor at that time.

In May 1889, a fire broke out, causing considerable damage to the fourth floor. There were established furniture makers using that floor of the building as an alternate location. They were C.J. Norquist, Lindblad Brothers and H.J. Newman. The third and part of the fourth floors was occupied by Hodgkins and Cadwell. The fire caused them great loss because this was their only location. The Weeks Company continued in business until about 1894 but may have developed into a retail store. Charles and his son are listed in the 1893 city directory as having a real estate office located at then 7 East Third Street. Weeks died on July 7, 1904, at the age of seventy.

ATLAS FURNITURE CO.

Date: 1887–1941
Location: Allen Street Extension
Founders: Lawrence E. Erickson, Frank O. Strandberg and Charles A. Johnson
Products: bedroom furniture

Atlas Furniture was established in 1883 as the Swedish Furniture Company. The original founders were Lawrence E. Erickson and Gustave Holmberg. In 1887, after the company moved from Jamestown to Randolph, New York, it incorporated as Atlas Furniture. At that time, about fifteen new stockholders were admitted. The operating officers of the company were Lawrence E. Erickson, Frank O. Strandberg and Charles A. Johnson. Holmberg relinquished an active part in the company due to the distance from his home in Frewsburg to the Randolph plant.

Charles A. Johnson was born in Sweden in 1860. At the age of twenty-two, he arrived in the United States and went directly to Jamestown, where his brother was already living and working. In 1882, Johnson began his business career working at Jamestown Banding Company. He remained there for five years, moving his employment to Atlas Furniture in 1887.

In the early years, Johnson divided much of his time between work and continuing his education by going to night school and studying at home. As with most of the Swedish settlers, learning the English language occupied much of his time. He was made a director of the board of Atlas in 1889

Atlas Furniture. *Courtesy of Fenton History Center.*

Atlas Furniture Plant 2. *Jamestown, New York, Historical and Industrial Review,* 1911.

and was also in charge of the finishing and shipping department. Johnson became a vice-president of the company in 1896.

In 1891, Atlas moved back to Jamestown. Three of the stockholders— Axel Anderson, John A. Burch and Claus Wahlgren—retired from Atlas and remained in Randolph to start another furniture company in the old Atlas Building. Atlas built a large modern facility with two four-story structures and a total floor space of 140,000 square feet. This new plant on Allen Street Extension was enlarged as required until 1910. At that time, Atlas purchased the Liberty Furniture Plant, a five-story building with 100,000 square feet of floor space located at then 11–15 Blackstone Avenue. Both plants had the advantage of a railroad siding, which was used for shipments of incoming lumber and outgoing finished furniture.

In 1911, the main Atlas plant on Allen Street Extension employed about 180 workers, and the Liberty plant employed about 150. Sometime after 1915, the Liberty plant was sold. The building became part of the Dahlstrom's complex. That original building remained until 2012.

Atlas produced better grades of bedroom furniture, including dressers, chiffoniers and toilet tables made from walnut, mahogany and other fine woods. The fine-quality furniture produced by Atlas was marketed throughout the United States. In May 1911, Ralph W. Taylor became

Jamestown Chair Company. *Jamestown, New York, Historical and Industrial Review*, 1911.

secretary and treasurer of Atlas. Some years later, Taylor left and became an officer and owner of Jamestown Table Company.

In 1920, Atlas was the second-largest bedroom furniture producer in the country, employing about two hundred workers, with permanent exhibition rooms in the Norton Club building on East Second Street in Jamestown. The company had a large distribution, shipping its product throughout the United States. The operating officers of the company were President Frank O. Strandberg; Vice-president Charles A. Johnson and Secretary/Treasurer John A. Hagg. Elim Holmberg, the son of one of the founders, worked in the packing room of the company for a short time. He then moved on to become secretary of Jamestown Chair Company, as well as a partner in the downtown Jamestown business of Swanson, Holmberg Shoe Company. Atlas Furniture continued to be a major furniture manufacturer in Jamestown for years and became Crawford Furniture Company.

JAMESTOWN LOUNGE CO.

Date: 1888–1984
Location: then 38–58 Winsor Street
Founders: Theodore D. Hanchett, Lynn F. Cornell, Arthur H. Greenlund
and Hurley L. Phillips
Products: lounges, couches and upholstered furniture

By producing the highest grade of lounges, couches and upholstered furniture, the Jamestown Lounge Co. assumed a commanding position in the local furniture industry for much of the twentieth century. Theodore D. Hanchett, Lynn F. Cornell, Arthur H. Greenlund and Hurley L. Phillips founded the company in 1888, with a plant located at 38–58 Winsor Street.

Theodore Hanchett was born in 1847 and moved to Jamestown in 1849. Educated in city schools, he began his business career at Allen and Grandin Woolen Mills located on First Street. Later, he went to work for Breed and Johnson Company. After leaving there, he worked for James Robinson, an organ manufacture. Hanchett moved on again, and in 1883, he was listed as a foreman at Shearman Brothers. He became president of Jamestown Lounge in 1904 after Hurley Phillips died. Years later, he became the president of

Jamestown Veneer Works. He retired from business in 1913 and died in 1914 at the age of sixty-seven.

Hurley L. Phillips was born in 1856. He came to Jamestown at the age of fifteen and completed his education in the Jamestown public school system. He began his business career as a cattle buyer and shipper. In 1883, he became a member of Beman, Breed & Phillips. When the company changed owners in 1886, he became affiliated with William Maddox and Charles W. Morgan in the Phillips, Maddox Company. He sold out that interest and became a founding member of Jamestown Lounge in 1888. Phillips would become president of the company and held that position until his death in 1903 at age forty-seven.

Lynn F. Cornell was born in December 1862. Educated in the Randolph school system and at Chamberlain Institute, he came to Jamestown in 1880. He found employment as a bookkeeper for Jamestown Iron Works and then went to Wells and Witcomb Iron Works. He worked for a time at Shearman Brothers and, in 1885, went in with Beman, Breed & Phillips, staying with them until the company changed hands in 1886.

Arthur H. Greenlund was born in 1862. He was educated in the Jamestown school system, and at age seventeen, he took up the trade of a furniture carver and designer. In 1886, he was a traveling salesman and in 1888 became a founder of the Jamestown Lounge Co. while continuing to travel and sell. He would later become superintendent of manufacturing. In 1901, Jamestown Lounge was incorporated, and Greenlund became one of the vice-presidents. Arthur Greenlund died in October 1917 at the age of fifty-five.

In January 1900, after just twelve years of existence, the company incorporated with an

Arthur Greenland, Jamestown Lounge. *History of Chautauqua County and Its People*, 1921.

operating capital of $250,000, employing approximately two hundred workers. By 1911, it had four four-story buildings with a total of 150,000 square feet of manufacturing floor space. A grocery store was set up in one of the buildings, allowing employees to buy groceries such as fresh fruit, vegetables and canned meat at specified times during the workweek. The company remained in business until 1984, a total of ninety-six years. The building later became part of Crawford Furniture. It now stands empty.

O'CONNELL & QUIGLEY (J.F. O'CONNELL & CO.)

Date: 1888–1895
Location: first corner of Washington and Fourth Street
Founders: Andrew P. Quigley and John F. O'Connell
Products: hall furniture, parlor and library tables

Originally established in 1888 as O'Connell & Quigley, with Andrew P. Quigley and John F. O'Connell as founders, this shop was known for the manufacturing of hall furniture and parlor and library tables. In 1890, manufacturing was done in a building located at the 117–19 corners of Washington and Fourth Streets. The steam-operated plant was equipped with all the latest improved woodworking machines. It had offices and warerooms at 40–46 West First Street. The distribution area of its tables covered Pennsylvania, Ohio and the New England states, as well as New York State. In 1890, John Dschuden and William T. Marsh were brought in as partners, and the company name changed to J.F. O'Connell & Company. In 1891, this small furniture maker employed seventeen men and five traveling salesmen. By 1893, the company was listed as being located on Jones and Gifford Avenue. The company was sold to the newly established Jamestown Furniture Company in September 1893.

John O'Connell was born in Jamestown. He attended the Jamestown public schools. After completing his required education, John went to work for Jamestown Bedstead. Sometime after leaving Jamestown Bedstead, he worked for the Breed Company. After eight years there, he went to work at A.P. Olson. He left Olson in 1888 and became a co-founder of O'Connell & Quigley.

HODGKINS & CADWELL

Date: 1888–1901
Location: Brooklyn Square (C.W. Weeks Building)
Founders: John Cadwell and George M. Hodgkins
Products: tables

Longtime furniture makers John Cadwell and George M. Hodgkins established this furniture factory in 1888. John Cadwell was born in 1841. He came to Jamestown in 1872 at the age of thirty-one. In 1884, he, along with Anson A. Burlin, bought Jamestown Wood Seat Chair Company. The success of his business venture was evident. Cadwell's business acumen allowed him an active role in city development. He was one of the founders of the Chautauqua Lake Railway, which was later sold to the Broadhead family. Cadwell was also the last president of the board of trustees for the village of Jamestown. In 1886, as president of the village trustees, he was responsible for turning the Village of Jamestown over to the City of Jamestown trustees. He died in 1926 at the age of eighty-five.

The company's first location was in the C.W. Weeks frame building owned by George B. Ford. Previously, Hodgkins and Ford had a factory at

Cadwell Cabinet. *Illustrated History of Jamestown*, 1900.

that location. John Cadwell bought out Ford's interest when he retired from the business in 1888. A fire broke out in May 1889 in the Weeks wooden building. The shop of Hodgkins & Cadwell sustained heavy losses of $1,000 to $2,000. The firm moved into a rented space in the new brick Ford Building adjoining the Weeks Building at then 7 Forest Avenue. The basement area was previously occupied by H.J. Newman. In 1892, Hodgkins & Cadwell employed thirty-five skilled craftsmen. The shop produced finely crafted tables under the guidance and expertise of the owners. John's son, Eugene, and John's brother, Frank, joined the business as bookkeepers in 1893. The company moved to a location at then 117–23 Foote Avenue in May 1894 near the future 1898 location of Empire Furniture. Cadwell, while affiliated with Hodgkins in 1895 and 1896, had another shop located at 14–16 Steele Street. This small shop manufactured bank and office furniture. George M. Hodgkins was born on May 6, 1836, and died in 1911 at the age of seventy-five.

By 1896, Hodgkins & Cadwell's furniture venture had prospered and grown, employing approximately forty workers at an average wage of $1.75 per day. The Hodgkins & Cadwell Company was gone by 1901. The new listing at the Foote Avenue location was Cadwell Cabinet Company.

H.J. NEWMAN & CO.

Date: 1889–1899
Location: then 7 Forest Avenue (Ford Building)
Founder: Harry J. Newman
Products: cribs and cots

This furniture shop was first established as J.R. Newman Company in 1875. The company changed its name in 1889, two years after the death of the founder, Jared R. Newman. The company produced a high-grade wood mantel for local and out-of-town furniture factories. It was also known for manufacturing cribs and cots. In 1889, the company occupied part of the Ford Building at 7 Forest Avenue, but a fire forced it to move. In 1890, the company relocated to a two-story eleven- by forty-eight-foot building on Holmes Street. At that time, the company employed thirty-five workmen and one salesman traveling to locations in the tri-state area. In January 1893, F.A. Johnson and H.V. Herrick joined the company and later that year purchased the interest of Harry Newman. The company employed about forty-three craftsmen. By 1895, the company's name changed to Newman Manufacturing Company. In 1896, the average wage for the forty to fifty workmen was $1.75 per day. The company now had the capacity to produce approximately two thousand mantels per year. By 1899, the company was gone, probably failing due to the depression in the mid-1890s.

Chautauqua Upholstery Co.

Date: 1890–?
Location: then 108–10 East Third Street
Founders: Augustus T. Knorzer? and Henry T. Koerner?
Products: made-to-order parlor suites, chairs and rockers

Established in 1890 at then 108–10 East Third Street, this company manufactured fine, made-to-order parlor suites, chairs and rockers. It also may have started manufacturing a unique and ingeniously devised bed couch. The couch was arranged so that the lower section could be opened or closed like a bureau drawer. It was operated on rollers, something like a trundle bed. Both sections were arranged so the head or pillow portion could be elevated or lowered to a number of positions. The two men who invented this couch were Augustus T. Knorzer and Henry T. Koerner. This is all the information we have on this shop and on the invention.

Chautauqua Table & Cabinet Co.

Date: 1890?–1891?
Location: then 700 East Second Street
Founders: ?
Products: tables

This was another company that had very little written about it. It was built by Charles J. Norquist around 1890. It employed about twenty men at then 700 East Second Street. John S. Anderson was the first proprietor of this small shop. In 1891, it may have become Chautauqua Furniture Company.

JOHNSTON, LAWSON & CO.

Date: 1890–1894
Location: then 118 Foote Avenue
Founders: Charles A. Lawson and Johnston
Products: parlor and library tables

In 1890, Charles A. Lawson and a man named Johnston established this company at then 118 Foote Avenue. Its twenty skilled workmen built parlor and library tables. In 1891, the company was named Johnson, Lawson & Haman. It completed a new line of hall trees and three new styles of tables. By 1893, the company had grown to employee thirty skilled workmen. In April 1894, the company became known as Crescent Table Company.

MORGAN MANUFACTURING CO.

Date: 1890–1906
Location: then 3–7 Ashville Avenue (Fairmount Avenue)
Founders: Lewis C. Jagger and Charles W. Morgan
Products: parlor tables

Morgan Manufacturing was established in 1890, and from the outset, this company specialized in the production of fine parlor tables. The investors controlling most of the holdings were Lewis C. Jagger and Charles W. Morgan. In 1891, the company was located in a huge five-story 50- by 120-foot building at then 3–7 Ashville Avenue (later Fairmount Avenue). The structure's basement housed the steam boilers that powered the plant. After 1891, a 31-foot structure was added to house an additional boiler, an engine room and a dry kiln. In those early years, Morgan Company employed approximately 100 to 150 workers in a variety of departments.

The first floor of the main building held offices. The four-inch-thick second floor of the building housed machinery where the manufacturing was done. Because of the thick, heavy beams, not a tremor was felt when the machines were running. The third, fourth and fifth floors housed the assembly and finish areas. Most of the benchwork like framing and assembling the legs was done on the third floor. On the fourth floor, the tops were sent through the sanding process and the tables were then assembled. All of the frame finishing was done on the fifth floor of the building. This process consisted of staining, lacquering, touchup and trim.

In 1895, Jagger bought out the investment interest of Morgan and sold a portion of that interest to Allen Falconer. Though Charles Morgan was not affiliated with the company, the new owners retained the name Morgan Manufacturing. Tables made by Morgan could be found in most of the eastern United States. Morgan Manufacturing produced twenty-five to thirty thousand tables per year. Its workers were paid the furniture industry's standard rate of $1.75 per day.

In 1903, the officers of the company were Lewis C. Jagger, Allen Falconer and Frederick W. Sears. A well-known local investor, Cyrus Jones, purchased Falconer's investment interest in the company in 1906. Shortly after that, Morgan Manufacturing was reestablished under the name of Jamestown Table Company.

JAMESTOWN DESK CO.

Date: 1890–1903
Location: then 20–26 Steele Street
Founders: John Brandin and W.A. Warner
Products: roller door bookcases

This company was established in April 1890. The founders were John Brandin and W.A. Warner. In that year, Fredrick O. Crossgrove replaced John Brandin, and George O. Meridith acquired one-third interest in the company.

Its specialty was a roller door bookcase. Another unique portion of its business was the supplying of veneer backing for the back of tabletops and chairs and to use as drawer bottoms. The veneer backing was shipped to furniture companies throughout the eastern United States. In 1891, Warner

Nevitt Sprague. *Illustrated History of Jamestown,* 1900.

John D. Windsor. *Illustrated History of Jamestown,* 1900.

sold out his investment interest to the other partners of the company. In 1892, Jamestown Desk and another company, Crossgrove & Meridith, shared the same building at then 20–26 Steele Street. This may have been all part of Jamestown Desk. The company employed about thirty-five skilled workmen in 1893. The average wage at the time for the company was $1.50 per day. In 1895, Jamestown Desk moved into a building at then 54 Taylor Street. The structure was 50 by 125 feet with a finishing room 50 by 100 feet. T. Nevitt Sprague bought out the shares of George O. Meridith in 1896. By 1898, John D. Windsor and Sprague had bought out the shares of Fredrick O. Crossgrove, who in 1899 would become one of the founders and president of Star Furniture Company. By 1900, the controlling interest of the company was with Windsor and Sprague. In that same year, the company grew to approximately fifty skilled workmen.

By 1903, Jamestown Desk was out of business. The building may have become part of Diamond Furniture, a well-established table company formerly known as A.P. Olson.

MADDOX, BAILEY & CO.

Date: 1890–1906
Location: then 560 East Second Street
Founders: William Maddox, Edward C. Bailey and Clayton E. Bailey
Products: tables

This company was formed as a result of the liquidation of Morgan, Maddox & Company in 1890. Charles Morgan left the company to form Morgan Manufacturing Company. This left Maddox and Bailey to continue the business under the restructured name of Maddox, Bailey & Company. The operating officers in 1891 were William Maddox, Edward C. Bailey and Edward's son, Clayton E. Bailey. The shop was known for the production of wood- and marble-top tables. In March 1891, the furniture business of Maddox & Bailey relocated to the vacant Breed Buildings on Winsor and Willard Street. A fire destroyed the shop at then 560 East Second Street. The Breed Company, now known as Breed-Johnson Furniture, moved to a new building on Jones and Gifford Avenue near Hallock Street. In 1896, this company's workers were paid an average wage of $1.75 per day. The plant employed about 125 to 200 men and was considered a large furniture company. The company investors were split when Maddox left to form Maddox Table Company in 1898.

The Bailey owners formed a partnership with Cyrus E. Jones, a well-known local investor. The company name changed to Bailey Jones Company, and it remained on Winsor and Willard Street. In 1904, Jones left the company and became one of the investors and founders of Jamestown Table Company, the former Morgan Manufacturing Company. The

Cyrus Jones. *Illustrated History of Jamestown,* 1900.

Bailey-Jones Co. *Illustrated History of Jamestown*, 1900.

Baileys remained at the Winsor and Willard Street location, changing the name to Bailey Table Company.

CHAUTAUQUA FURNITURE CO.

Date: 1891–1899?
Location: Second Street
Founders: ?
Products: tables and desks

This company may have first been established in 1891 as Chautauqua Table and Cabinet. It manufactured tables and desks at a location that may have been on Second Street in East Jamestown. In 1899, the Jamestown City Directory has no listing for the company.

BENSON, HAND & FRISBEE

Date: 1892–mid 1890s?
Location: then 10–22 Steele Street
Founders: Junius H. Benson, William L. Hand and Beardsley R. Frisbee
Products: parlor tables

This furniture shop of fifteen employees was established in 1892. It may have bought up the interest of Nelson, Bergland & Company. The founders of the new company were Junius H. Benson, William L. Hand and Beardsley R. Frisbee. It manufactured parlor tables in a location at then 10–22 Steele Street.

The company did not last long and failed during the mid-1890s economic depression.

CRESCENT TABLE CO.

Date: 1894–1898
Location: then 118 Foote Avenue
Founders: Charles A. Lawson, Horace L. Rew and O.O. Rew
Products: parlor and library tables

Founders Charles A. Lawson, Horace L. Rew and O.O. Rew established Crescent Table in 1894. The shop was previously known as Johnston, Lawson & Company. Crescent was located at then 118 Foote Avenue, in a building shared by Curtis and Page Fancy Rockers, owned by Scott Page and Edwin W. Curtis. Crescent was a manufacture of parlor and library tables. The company was gone by 1898, and Empire Furniture may have absorbed the building.

EMPIRE FURNITURE CO.

Date: 1894–1953
Location: Chandler Street Extension
Founders: Frank O. Anderson, Peter F. Johnson and Charles N. Johnson
Products: chamber suites

Established in February 1894, Empire Furniture became another of the large furniture companies that started from small roots. For over sixty years, it was a contributing factor to the rich Jamestown furniture history. Frank O. Anderson was born in Sweden in 1870. Anderson's father, Anders Svenson, decided to change the family name to Anderson when they arrived in the United States in 1889. In his native country, Frank learned the cabinetmaker's trade. Upon his arrival in Jamestown at the age of eighteen, he found work at A.C. Norquist Company for seventy-five cents a day, working six days a week. Anderson established Empire Furniture Company in 1894.

Founded by Frank O. Anderson, Peter F. Johnson and Peter's brother Charles N. Johnson, this shop commenced operations in a rented building on Chandler Street that may have been owned by the Norquists. The owners and six to eight workmen started building chamber suites, producing approximately one or two a day, or about thirty a month. In the beginning, the wood craftsman and his skilled hand were the only machines in the rented building. As the business grew and became more successful, the need for a larger building was recognized. In 1898, Empire moved into a five-story structure located at then 142 Foote Avenue; it remained there for the next fifty-five years.

In 1900, the need for a financial secretary and office manager was filled by the appointment of Charles J. Norquist, another skilled furniture businessman coming from one of the founding families of furniture making in Jamestown.

As Empire's prosperity continued, two large additions were constructed at the Foote Avenue site in 1900. With the increase in facilities, thirty to forty chamber suites could be produced in a day, or one suite every eighteen minutes, with a workforce of approximately seventy-five men using the latest improved labor-saving machinery.

In 1900, Frank O. Anderson was superintendent and general manager of Empire. All of the firm's officers were practical men with varied degrees of furniture making and successful business operation who took an active part in Empire and the continued success of the company.

In November 1904, construction of another new structure began in an adjoining lot next to the main plant. This building was a five-story frame building sixty-five by sixty-five feet. It was completed in December and used for storage and as a finishing plant. By 1911, Empire employed from 175 to 200 skilled workers, specializing in the building of high-quality grades of bedroom furniture, including a complete line of chiffoniers and odd dressers in a wide variety of attractive designs from mahogany and choice native woods.

Frank Anderson is also listed as the owner of the company that for a short time around 1912 manufactured pedestals and tabourets at his Empire plant. In 1914, with the astounding growth, weekly output was $14,000. The company controlled the entire process from log to the finished product. Anderson was an ingenious man due to his inventive nature, designing the labor-saving machinery in the plant. The woodworking machines and specialty equipment maintained Empire's long-standing reputation for the production of a high-quality product. One of those machines was used to make dovetails for the construction of drawer and cabinet corners. The company reorganized in 1912, becoming Empire Case Goods Company. Anderson remained the president of the company until his retirement in 1925, when he turned the business over to his son, Paul N. Anderson.

During the Great Depression, Empire employees who had been laid off worked for room and board as they built the former Traynor and Winter Restaurant (now the Bemus Inn) and cabins (no longer extant) in Bemus Point. Empire also furnished these cabins. Joanna Traynor Winter remembers going to visit her father's office at Empire as a child.

She was fascinated with a small mouse that lived in his desk drawer and survived on bits of his sandwiches. She remembers the enclosed walkway that crossed Foote Avenue and connected with Empire buildings on Foote Avenue near Water Street. The company remained in business until 1953, and in 1954, the buildings on Foote Avenue were torn down.

FRANK O. ANDERSON (IN RETIREMENT)

When Anderson retired from active business life in 1925, his time was devoted to the city of Jamestown. One of his many projects was raising money for the building of the Hotel Jamestown on the corner of Third and Cherry Streets. The Hotel Jamestown was one of three large hotels that sparked Anderson's entrepreneurial interest. The others were the Hotel Samuels located on the corner of Third and Cherry Streets and the Humphrey House located at then 15–23 South Main Street in Brooklyn Square. These three hotels were built during the heyday of the Jamestown Furniture Exposition to accommodate furniture buyers and sellers from all over the United States. Jamestown hosted this exposition twice a year for many years, commencing in 1917 with the completion of the Furniture Mart Building located at the corner of Washington and Second Streets. Anderson was responsible for raising millions of dollars for the Hotel Jamestown Corporation. In November 1960, an article appeared in the *Jamestown Post Journal* written by Jennie Vimmerstedt praising the efforts of the committee.

After the 1906 San Francisco earthquake, Anderson packed his luggage and left for that city, returning with a full list of furniture orders. He knew the Swedish craftsmen in his plant could turn out the furniture needed to replace ruined furniture in the homes and hotels of San Francisco at below anyone else's cost, even if the furniture needed was not part of his present furniture line. This action reflects Anderson's resourcefulness as a businessman and his benevolence in the face of adversity. Frank O. Anderson died in April 1945.

Munson & Waite Co.

Date: 1895–1904
Location: then 710–12 East Second and Winsor Street
Founders: Charles F. Munson and Charles M. Waite
Products: wood mantels

Established in 1895, this shop's investors were Charles F. Munson and Charles M. Waite. The company had previously been owned and operated under E.A. Ross & Son, established in 1891. The Ross family was noted for sawmills operating outside Jamestown, in the area now known as Ross Mills. Charles Morris Waite was born in March 1855 in Poland, New York. He was in charge of office affairs at Munson & Waite Company and remained with the business only two years after its establishment. Charles Munson was from Kane, Pennsylvania. Before coming to Jamestown, Munson had been

Munson & Waite Building. *Illustrated History of Jamestown*, 1900.

in charge of the construction department at Pullman Palace Car Company located in Pullman, Illinois. While there, he became a skilled mechanic. Upon his arrival in Jamestown, he worked for a time at Breed-Johnson furniture. After leaving there, he established Munson & Waite and was in charge of manufacturing.

Munson & Waite Company was located at then 710–12 East Second and Winsor Streets. The building measured 40 by 115 feet with three stories and a double basement. The building had wings that housed dry kilns and a powerhouse. The firm employed approximately thirty skilled workmen in 1900 at an average wage of $1.50 per day. It was considered to be a medium-sized furniture shop, producing wood mantels for the building trades using the best grades of hardwoods. This product was marketed locally and outside the area by two traveling salesmen armed with blueprint illustrations to demonstrate their wares.

In 1904, nine years after Munson & Waite had taken control, the company was reestablished as Munson & Johnson Company. During World War I, it built wood propellers.

JAMESTOWN VENEER WORKS

Date: 1895–1903
Location: then 18–20 Steele Street
Founders: George E. Griffith and Frank Cadwell
Products: veneer strips for furniture industry

This factory was one of many shops manufacturing veneers for the furniture industry, with the bulk of its customers located in Jamestown. The job of cutting veneer strips almost as thin as paper and in any length from a variety of choice woods was its specialty. The woods used in the production of veneer were Birdseye, blister and curl maple, plain and fancy birch, oak and ash, as well as other native woods.

In 1895, George E. Griffith and Frank Cadwell established Jamestown Veneer Works. The shop operated under the company name George E. Griffith Company for a brief period. In 1897, Griffith and Cadwell sold out to a new group of investors: Burton R. Pratt, George B. Peterson and Austin J. Thayer. Charles E. Fisk and Nathan M. Willson were added as partners later that year. Charles E. Fisk was born in Ellington, New York, in

February 1863. In 1870, the family moved to a farm two and a half miles from Fluvanna, New York. Later, they moved again, settling in Gerry, New York. Fisk attended public schools and went on to Ellington Academy. Upon graduation, he went to work for Milton Farguson operating creameries throughout Chautauqua and Cattaraugus Counties. Accepting a job with Strong Veneer Company, he left Farguson creameries. Strong was located in Gerry. He remained there for ten years, becoming well versed in the operations of the business and rising to a good position in the company. But Fisk would leave Strong Veneer and the area, moving to Grand Rapids and accepting a position as superintendent of the Grand Rapids Company, followed by eighteen months of service as superintendent of the Welsh Dixford Veneer Company.

In 1897, Fisk returned to Jamestown, forming a partnership with other investors to establish Jamestown Veneer Works. The factory was located at then 18–20 Steele Street in a three-story building sixty-five by sixty-five feet. In 1896, the company employed six men at a wage of $1.75 per day.

Shortly after 1900, Pratt retired from the business. The officers were George B. Peterson, Austin J. Thayer and Nathan M. Willson. The shop

Pearl City Veneer Company. *Jamestown, New York, Historical and Industrial Review*, 1911.

now employed ten men at its Steele Street location. Around 1903, the company name changed to Pearl City Veneer. Veneer panels are made of thin sheets of wood stripped from the fallen trees. Some of the common woods used in the Jamestown area were maple, birch, oak and ash. These sheets are "sandwiched" together or plied together and glued. A three- or five-ply panel has its sheets glued at right angles to one another. As you look between the layers, you will see the plies. The glues were waterproof, and layering the sheets at right angles gave strength to the panels. These veneers, used as accents in tables, dining room furniture and other pieces, lent to the beauty of the furniture piece. They were also used in the production of door panels because of their strength and the fact that they held up under damp conditions, keeping the door from warping.

JAMESTOWN FURNITURE CO.

Date: ?–1904
Location: foot of West Main Street
Founders: Charles F. Dschuden?
Products: parlor tables and desks

F.M. Curtis Company. *Jamestown, New York, Historical and Industrial Review*, 1911.

The established date of this company is not known, but in 1876, a Jamestown Furniture Company located at the foot of West Main Street burned down. Mrs. Ezra Wood owned it. She also owned Wood & Company in the same building. In 1893, the *Jamestown Evening Journal* lists the purchase of John F. O'Connell Company by the newly established Jamestown Furniture. The president of the company was Charles F. Dschuden.

In 1900, the company produced parlor tables and desks on Jones and Gifford Avenue. The building was owned and occupied by Breed-Johnson furniture. In

1901, the president of the company was Henry F. Sampson, and the secretary and treasurer was listed as Clarence A. Anderson. In 1903–4, the company was located on East Second Street and the president was F.M. Curtis. In 1905–6, there is no listing for the company, and F.M. Curtis is in that location.

BAILEY, JONES CO.

Date: 1898–1911
Location: then 105 Winsor Street
Founders: Clayton E. Bailey, Edward C. Bailey and Cyrus E. Jones
Products: parlor and library tables

In 1898, the Maddox, Bailey Company was established as Bailey, Jones Company when William Maddox left the company and investor Cyrus E. Jones was brought in. The officers of the newly established company were now Clayton E. Bailey, Edward C. Bailey and Cyrus E. Jones. Remaining at their Winsor Street address, they continued the production of parlor and library tables. In 1900, Bailey, Jones incorporated with upward of three hundred employees, making it one of the largest furniture shops in Jamestown.

In 1906, Jones left the company and became one of the investors and founders of Jamestown Table Company located near the boat landing. The company retained its name Bailey, Jones Company until 1912, when it changed to Bailey Table Company.

Carl L. Liedblad. *History of Chautauqua County and Its People*, 1921.

In 1909, the officers of the company were President Clayton Bailey and Vice-president Benjamin M. Bailey. The secretary was listed as Albert Gilbert, and the treasurer was Charles L. Liedblad.

MADDOX TABLE CO.

Date: 1898–1984
Location: 101–25 Harrison Street
Founder: William Maddox
Products: tables

William Maddox was one of the most respected furniture makers and inventors in the history of the Jamestown furniture industry. He was born in 1856, and his great-uncle was a brother of Ethan Allen. Maddox finished school and served an apprenticeship at Gunter, Hull & Parker, a furniture manufacture in Scranton, Pennsylvania. He became a skilled cabinetmaker. Maddox's skills were not limited to cabinetmaking. While in Scranton, he invented a reclining rocking chair. In 1885, he moved the manufacturing of this chair to Jamestown.

In 1891, Maddox patented one of the most important machines at that time in furniture manufacturing. It was the first machine to sand, rub and polish a wood tabletop. This stroke polisher outdid hand polishing one hundred to one in a dozen ways. In 1891, he patented the machine. It could be set up and operated in a space only eight feet square and required only one horsepower to run. It ran without noise or vibration, so it did not have to be fastened to the floor, which made for easier relocation. It could take stock five feet square and twelve inches thick and rework it into a fine tabletop. The machine could adjust itself to any uneven or warped surface. Eventually, Maddox patented and perfected twenty-one different woodworking production machines and established a company in Jamestown to make and sell them worldwide.

This amazing businessman, inventor and community leader died in 1936 at the age of eighty in his home, which is now the Jamestown Boys and Girls Club.

For over eighty-six years, Maddox Table was one of the most successful furniture companies in Jamestown. Established in 1898 in a newly constructed factory at then 101–25 Harrison Street, it was the most modern furniture factory in Jamestown. Fine exotic mahogany and native woods produced parlor, library and office tables, which constituted the early success of the company. It had over 150 designs of parlor and library tabourets and buffet pedestals. Later, it would expand its furniture line to include dining room suites. In 1900, during peak production hours, the company could build one table per minute. At that time, Maddox employed 225 skilled workmen in various departments. By 1911, the company had grown to over 350 to 400

Maddox Table Building. *Courtesy of Fenton History Center.*

skilled workmen. Two large three-story buildings covered two acres of land at the Harrison Street location.

The manufacturing plant was 135 by 100 feet in dimension. Behind the manufacturing building was a switch siding from the Erie Railroad main tracks. Another 100- by 150-foot building housed the office and warehouse. In a number of smaller buildings, the company had dry kilns, a fireproof engine, a boiler and a pump room. Its 90-foot smokestack and sprawling complex of buildings could be seen from many of the city's hill locations.

Maddox shipped fine-quality furniture to all parts of the United States, England, Australia, Japan and Denmark. In 1900, shipments were even made to China. A unique device used by the sales staff was a twenty-five- by thirty-one- by nine-inch box containing three full-size tables, the largest being twenty-four inches square. These were patented knockdown parlor tables. This sales tool allowed the salesmen to show the quality workmanship of Maddox Table products to customers all over the world.

In collaboration with Jamestown Aristotype, Maddox invented a quick method machine for turning out photo prints. This allowed salesmen to make

=MADDOX SPECIAL=

Set up designs knocked down.
A system of Bolts and Locks.
No glue required. Simple but rigid.

Patented for the benefit of Maddox
Table Co. and Dealers only.

Above: Maddox knockdown table. *Courtesy of Fenton History Center.*

Left: Burton Maddox. *Courtesy of Fenton History Center.*

enough copies for a catalogue and show the complete line of furniture made by Maddox Table Company. It was also the first company in the industry to trademark furniture stamping (MAD-OX) on all of its products. The company's success was due solely to its founder, William Maddox. Milton H. Clark, one of the owners of Clark Hardware Company, was born in 1850. He also invested in the Maddox Table Company. He died in July 1911 at the age of sixty-one.

Charles W. Herrick assisted in the development, management and organization of Maddox Table. Herrick was born in Jamestown in 1867 and, upon completion of school, became part of the banking industry in Jamestown, rising to the position of vice-president. Herrick was also the treasurer of Maddox until January 1910, when he became the senior investor and founder of C.W. Herrick Manufacturing Company, another furniture factory in Falconer, New York. Herrick died in 1932.

In 1919, Maddox was sold and became part of Shearman Brothers. However, the Maddox name was retained. With this acquisition, Shearman Brothers became the largest furniture employer in Jamestown.

A tornado touched down in the Jamestown area on June 10, 1945, tearing off two stories of Maddox's main manufacturing building. The company recovered and continued to fill customer orders. In 1978, Crawford's Furniture (previously Atlas) purchased Maddox Table. This company was gone by 1984, ending another early furniture maker important to Jamestown's growth and the second-largest furniture manufacture in the United States.

Burton Maddox, the son of William, started as a shipping clerk and in later years ran the machine shop. Burton was known as the youngest furniture manufacturer to show at the Grand Rapids, Michigan furniture exposition in 1907. At that exposition, he displayed toy dollhouse chairs and tables made from pieces of wood at his father's factory. This dollhouse furniture was of the highest quality and workmanship. Burton died in 1965.

MADDOX MACHINE CO.

This company that was started by William Maddox and at the outset was called the William Maddox Machine Company deserves mention because of the impact Maddox's machines had on the furniture industry. Maddox Machine was first located in a portion of the Maddox Table complex on Harrison Street.

Maddox Table machine. *Courtesy of Fenton History Center.*

In 1926, it relocated to 61–63 South Main Street. The premiere machine made by Maddox was a rubbing, sanding and polishing machine that revolutionized furniture manufacturing by all but eliminating the need for hand sanding on parlor tables. That machine would sand hardwoods and all kinds of figured veneers; it could also do coarse rubbing, fine rubbing and rotten stone work in such a manner that most skillful hand rubbers could not equal. It was so reliable that Maddox Table had seven of its nine machines in 1900 running constantly for over one year without any interruptions.

CADWELL CABINET CO.

Date: 1899–1915
Location: first at Institute Street and Holmes Street
Founders: John and Eugene Cadwell
Products: office and bank furniture, telephone booths, blackboards and
    battery boxes

This shop was established in 1899 by founders John and his son Eugene Cadwell. The company was listed at the rear of then 125 Institute and Holmes Streets. Star Furniture Company would later occupy this location. In 1901, the shop moved to then 123 Foote Avenue in a building located on the east side of Foote Avenue across the street from Empire Furniture. From 1901 to 1906, John's brother Frank Cadwell was listed as the owner of Special Furniture Company, located in the same building.

Cadwell Cabinet produced cabinets, office and bank furniture, telephone booths, blackboards and battery boxes. In 1915, Cadwell added two partners to the company. The name then changed to Cadwell, Vernon Company. Eugene Cadwell was born in 1870 and died in 1952 at the age of eighty-two.

STAR FURNITURE CO.

Date: 1899–1939
Location: then 40–44 Steele Street
Founders: Fredrick O. Crossgrove and J.E. Hall
Products: bookcases and dressers

In 1899, Star Furniture was at then 40–44 Steele Street. This company began by manufacturing a medium-priced line of bookcases and dressers. The officers of Star in 1900 were Fredrick O. Crossgrove and J.E. Hall. They employed approximately twenty-five skilled workers. By 1901, Star had moved to then 25–37 Briggs Street. In later years, it expanded to cover nearly the entire block surrounded by Institute, Briggs and Holmes Streets. Pearl City Veneer occupied the plant on Steele Street in 1903.

Star incorporated in 1901 and listed its new operating officers as President and Treasurer Jay Crissey. Jay Crissey was born in Stockton, New York, in 1861. He attended Fredonia public schools and graduated from Fredonia State. Upon completion of his education, he became a teacher. For twenty years he worked at that profession, serving nine of those twenty years as principal of Belmont, New York High School. He served one year as a faculty member of Central City Normal School in Chicago and the remaining years until 1900 as superintendent of schools in Penn Yan, New York. In 1901, he invested in Star Furniture, becoming president of that successful furniture maker. He died in 1925.

In 1910, Star Furniture Company and Banner, another furniture company, suffered a loss at the Grand Rapids, Michigan Furniture Exposition. A fire broke out in one of the buildings where their furniture exhibits were stored.

In 1915, Star purchased Williamson Veneer Company located on Briggs Street near the main factory of Star Furniture. In 1920, Jay Crissey was listed as president, with two other members of the family listed as officers. Anna L. Crissey was vice-president, and the second vice-president was Mary R. Crissey. Henry P. Robertson held the position of secretary. He was one of the buyers of Jamestown Bedstead

Scott Baker. *History of Chautauqua County and Its People*, 1921.

in 1904. The treasurer was Scott Baker, a descendant of the early founding Baker family.

Scott Baker was born in Jamestown in August 1876. He attended Jamestown public schools and Jamestown Business College. Once out into the busy world of business in Jamestown, he had no problem finding work. He first worked for the Erie Railroad Company as a clerk. Moving from the clerk's office, he found positions available in the furniture industry. He worked in an executive capacity at Atlas Furniture and at Bailey, Jones Company. In 1904, he was offered a position as secretary at Star Furniture.

The Baker family was well known in Jamestown. Scott's grandfather Henry was a founder and had acquired an extensive amount of real estate. The Baker family donated land that would become Baker Park. It was the first large public park in the city of Jamestown, located between Fourth and Fifth Streets near the Ironstone Restaurant.

Star's specialty line of furniture in the 1920s was bedroom suites and washstands, but like many of the other furniture shops, other lines were offered. In 1939, forty-one years after it was founded, its building burned and was never rebuilt.

CABINET SHOPS WITH ONLY A BRIEF HISTORY

Many of the early cabinet shops were small family-owned businesses with only brief histories. This may have been due to the lack of funds to mechanize and develop new and faster manufacturing techniques for their existing and new products. Some of the companies that succeeded are listed in the Jamestown City Directories. These directories began in 1875 and continue to this day. Every year is not always represented, and even though conflicting information may appear, the directories are invaluable for historical research.

C.C. Sterns was listed only in 1875 and was a manufacture of extension tables.

Marsh and Firman are listed in the 1883 directory. They may have been established prior because a fire is listed in 1881. The last listing was in 1886.

Swanson, Bergquist & Company and J.M. Beman are listed only in the 1884 directory.

Chautauqua Novelty was established in 1883, and W.C. Cise was the proprietor in 1890.

Orrin Applequist is listed as a manufacture of desks in the 1893 directory. Fenton, Robertson & Company was a manufacture of sideboards located in east Jamestown. This company is listed for approximately two years.

Lucius N. Willard, located on Winsor Street, manufactured coat racks, towel racks and folding hat racks. It is found only in the 1888 and 1893 directories.

Jamestown Parlor Table Company is listed as a manufacture of tables located at 1026 East Second Street from 1898 to 1900. The owners were Peter Shelberg and Fred A. Johnson.

Chautauqua Desk Company on Jones and Gifford Avenue is listed in 1895 and once more in 1899; it made desks and bookcases.

Appleby & Erickson Company made parlor and library tables and is listed only once in the 1899 city directory.

In 1906, the city directory listed Standard Furniture Company as a manufacture of parlor tables located on West Fourth Street.

Art Furniture Company at 516 West Fourth Street is listed only once in 1907. This was the location of the old Martyn Brothers Company.

William A. Warren manufactured tables at 52 Hazzard Street from 1909 to 1912.

Chris Marker & Son is listed as a pedestal and tabourets manufacturer in 1912 and was located at 192 South Main Street.

The Acme Novelty Works at 516 West Fourth Street and Mission Novelty Works at 352 South Main Street were two companies listed in the 1913 city directory. The Acme Novelty Works made folding tables and novelties. The Mission Novelty Works made chairs and novelties. The Mission Novelty Works is listed in the directories up through 1922, but Acme only appears up to 1916.

Chautauqua Chair Company moved from Sherman, New York, in 1915 and is listed only in the 1916 city directory. Located at 16–24 Steele Street, this company manufactured specialty bedroom and dining room chairs. It applied for receivership in 1916.

From 1914 to 1920, the Strong Veneer Company

American Carving Works.
Jamestown, New York, Historical and Industrial Review, 1911.

located at 321 Washington Street was a branch office and contained sample rooms for the main plant located in Gerry, New York.

Paterniti Table Company located at 213 Hopkins Avenue appears in 1920 and once again in 1922.

Jamestown Carving located at 510–14 Crescent Street is listed only in 1922.

Chapter 5

Jamestown, the Second-Largest Producer of Wood Furniture in the United States

1900

THE TWENTIETH CENTURY AND THE BUSINESS OF WOOD

At the beginning of the twentieth century, the city of Jamestown was a busy, bustling community. The municipal light plant supplied power to the 1,200-candlepower arc streetlights. Street railway lines surrounded every section of the city extending east and west, bringing close the villages of Falconer, Celoron and Lakewood. The principal business streets were no longer muddy ruts or dusty dirt roads but were paved with brick made in East Jamestown. More than two hundred manufacturers produced a variety of goods representing the industrial strength of Jamestown.

Jamestown industries were the heart of the economy, employing more than seven thousand workers with a total annual wage of approximately $3 million. Four major industries generated most of that revenue: wood furniture manufacturing, photographic paper production, worsted fabric mills and metal furniture manufacturing like commercial office furniture.

At that time, Jamestown was known as New York State's industrial city among similar-sized cities in the state. The factors required to achieve this title included the number of factories per capital, amount of invested capital, number of wage earners and value of its products. During that time, Jamestown was the second-largest furniture producer in the United States; only Grand Rapids, Michigan, was larger.

These first three companies are examples of small wood shops with rather short and confusing business lives. These companies flourished for a short time, moved, reestablished, went out of business and disappeared for a time only to reappear in a new location or in a building with other companies. This scenario was true of small shops with limited capital to spend on more modern machinery, larger facilities and higher wages for better-trained employees.

FINLEY MANUFACTURING CO.

Date: 1900–1910
Location: then 50 Steele Street
Founder: P. Anson Finley
Products: kitchen tables, ironing boards and a variety of miscellaneous furniture

This company is first listed in the 1900 Jamestown City Directory, with P. Anson Finley as the founder. In 1903, a new plant at then 50 Steele Street was constructed. Finley occupied the plant along with Nelson & Company and Jamestown Art and Carving Company, two other furniture makers. Finley produced a variety of wood products, with kitchen tables and ironing boards as specialty items in the early years.

In 1904, Finley Manufacturing was located on Steele Street, and Anson was still listed as the proprietor. In 1906, the company produced a high-quality line of chiffoniers. The company's president was P.A. Finley, C.E. Strong was secretary and Owen Finley was treasurer.

The business disappeared in 1910, and the city directory lists a Columbia M.F.G. Company at the Steele Street location.

WARD CABINET CO.

Date: 1900–1914
Location: then 518 West Fourth Street
Founders: Michael W. Ward and A.S. Ward
Products: office and store furniture

The Ward Cabinet Company is first listed in the 1900 city directory. The small shop was located at then 518 West Fourth Street in one of the buildings owned by the Martyn Brothers. The Ward shop was small and at the time produced office and store furniture. The owners of the company were Michael W. Ward and A.S. Ward, relatives of the Martyn family.

Michael W. Ward was active in Republican politics and the Martyn Fire Company. He was related to Marius and George Martyn, owners of the former Martyn Lounge Company, where he had worked prior to starting his own business. He died on February 7, 1918. By 1906, the shop was under the ownership of M.W. Ward. The company shared a location in one of the Fourth Street buildings with Golden Furniture. A fire caused great damage to the Ward business in July 1906. In 1912, the name changed again to M.W. & C.S. Ward Company, adding Cathleen S. Ward as a partner in the company. By 1914, M.W. & C.S. Ward Company was gone.

BRODEN TABLE CO.

Date: 1901–1946
Location: then 714 West Second Street
Founders: Axel and Herman Broden
Products: tables

This company first appeared in the 1901 Jamestown City Directory and was located at then 714 West Second Street. The founders of the company were Axel and Herman Broden. By 1904, the small shop had moved to the rear of a building located at then 100 Steele Street. In 1908, Chadakoin Furniture and Brodine occupied the building at 100 Steele Street. In 1910, no listing appears for Broden (Brodine) Table Company. In 1920, Brodin (Broden, Brodine) is listed in the city directory as a maker of library tables at 75 Steele Street. In 1922, Herman Brodin is the proprietor of Brodin Manufacturing Plant, and Axel is listed as a woodworker at the plant.

The Broden/Brodine/Brodin Company was gone by 1946. Herman Brodin died in January 1949.

UNION FURNITURE CO. (UNION NATIONAL FURNITURE)

Date: 1901–1994
Location: then 226 Crescent Street
Founders: August, Edward and Alfred Nord
Products: bookcases, desks, china cabinets, buffets and tables

Union Furniture was a result of the successful business venture of the Nord and Norquist families. The company was established in 1901 and remained in business for ninety-three years. The Nord brothers came to this country, and all went to work for their cousin at A.C. Norquist Company. Responding to the entrepreneurial drive that motivated a number of the Swedish immigrants, the four brothers went on to open a retail furniture store located on East Second Street. As the business grew, a larger shop was built close to the first location. Two of the brothers, John and Edward, were the sales force, while August delivered the furniture in a horse-drawn wagon. John, the eldest Nord, was born in Sweden in 1865. He came to Jamestown at the age of seventeen in July 1882. Upon arriving in Jamestown, he immediately went to work in the carving room of his cousin's factory, A.C. Norquist Company.

In 1901, three of the four Nord brothers left the retail business, seeing greater profits in manufacturing furniture. Selling out their interest to their older brother, John, and with cash from an inheritance, they were able to accumulate approximately $10,000 to start production on a high-grade dining room suite.

With a staff of eight men, including the owners, manufacturing operations began in a small building at then 226 Crescent Street. This site was formerly used to manufacture bicycle handlebars. The first articles of furniture were bookcases and desks. In that first year of production, Union marketed $10,000 worth of bookcases and desks, with individual prices ranging from $25 to $50. It expanded its line to include china cabinets, buffets and tables.

In those early years, August Nord was president and superintendent of the company; secretary, treasurer and general manager was Edward Nord; and vice-president was Alfred A. Nord, who served as overseer of the cabinet department. Frank O. Norquist, a cousin of the Nords, was also an officer. August F. Nord came to Jamestown in 1885. He traveled from Smoland, Sweden, where he was born in 1868. He first went to work in the finishing department of A.C. Norquist Company and remained there for eleven years. Edward C. Nord was born in Sweden in 1871 and

¶ It is characteristic of the Anglo-Saxon that his home shall be his castle, a place embodying all the refinements and luxury of modern ideals. It is also characteristic of the progressive business man that he seeks always to provide those things demanded by the public. ¶ A visit to our store reveals to what extent this establishment has gone to supply the wants of the luxury-loving as well as those whose purse will permit only the substantial necessities in the furniture line. We carry a large and up-to-date stock of everything belonging to a first-class furniture store.

Nord   Furniture   Company

109-111 East Second St.   Jamestown, New York

Nord Furniture Company. *Courtesy of Fenton History Center.*

came to Jamestown in 1891. He went to work at A.C. Norquist Company, starting out in the machine and carving department. Alfred A. Nord was born in 1875 and came to Jamestown in 1891 with his brother Edward. He found work at A.C. Norquist Company in the hand-carving department.

Sound marketing and manufacturing practices paid back with increased volume. The need to modernize their equipment and enlarge the building became pressing in order to remain competitive in the changing furniture industry. One of the company's early equipment improvements was to change from belt-driven machines to electric motor drives on each machine. This greatly improved the efficiency of the process.

In 1904, the company incorporated under the laws of New York State. It was one of many prominent furniture makers in the city of Jamestown, employing 175 to 300 workers during its peak production periods. In 1920, the need for increased output was again recognized, and a large five-story brick addition of 100,000 square feet was built next to the original 65,000-square-foot wooden building. The two buildings took on the shape of a U and more than doubled the size of the plant.

In November 1924, a fire broke out in the dry kilns and nearby lumber piles, endangering the main factory. Due to the quick action of the workers and fire company, the business was saved—but not before an estimated $100,000 in damage was done.

In 1925, Alldor, son of August, joined the company as assistant manager of National Furniture, a branch company. In 1929, Wesley, son of Alfred Nord, joined the company as a cost accountant at the Union plant. Those were not the only additions in the 1920s. August's daughter Gladys joined the company in 1925 after graduating from Wellesley College.

Following a lengthy labor dispute in 1940, the company combined with National Furniture, another local furniture shop located on Blackstone Avenue and owned by the Nord family. The company became known as Union National Furniture.

Union National closed its doors in 1994 and was demolished in March 1997.

FIRES!

Fires were a constant threat to the furniture shops. Most of the early buildings were wood frame, and when a fire broke out, the building could be totally engulfed before any fire company could reach it. Paints, varnishes, lacquers and stains posed a problem due to the volatile state of the liquid and fumes when exposed to heat. Spontaneous combustion was a problem with rags saturated with these liquids if not properly disposed of in an outside metal container. Heated sawdust from machines running for long periods would lie in smoldering piles in danger of igniting if not disposed of properly. Companies made an effort to reduce the spread of fire by placing the finishing departments on the top floor of a building. The reason behind this idea was if a fire did break out, it could be contained to that top floor. That way of thinking was not foolproof, and many a cabinet shop burned down in an all-consuming fire.

Fire hit the Breed Factory on Willard and Winsor Street in 1888. Jamestown Table Company in 1903, Breed and Johnson in 1904, Empire Furniture in 1904, Jamestown Veneer Company in 1905, Himebaugh in 1906, Standard Table Company in 1923 and Monarch Furniture in 1924 were also damaged by fire.

PEARL CITY VENEER CO.

Date: 1901–1924
Location: then 40–42 Steele Street
Founders: Theodore Hanchett, Charles E. Fisk and Nathan M. Willson
Products: veneer panels for dining tables and bedroom furniture

An allied industry to furniture factories was the production and sale of veneers and veneer panels. These panels were used as inlays and accents in tables and dining and bedroom furniture. Pearl City Veneer Company was one of these suppliers. Established in 1901 and incorporated in 1903, the company was formerly known as Jamestown Veneer Works, established in 1895. Theodore Hanchett, a founder of Jamestown Lounge Company, was president. Charles E. Fisk was the vice-president, having been a partner with Jamestown Veneer Works. Nathan M. Willson, another partner at the former company, was secretary and treasurer. In 1903, the company was located in a building with Jamestown Turning Works at then 40–42 Steele Street. By 1911, the building also housed Nelson Company and Jamestown Carving.

Pearl City produced three- and five-ply panels of veneer in plain and figured stock, glass backings, end and door panels and drawer bottoms available in all colors and grains of wood. By 1911, the company occupied two large three-story buildings with approximately twelve thousand square feet of floor space and a workforce of fifty men in various departments. All of the most up-to-date equipment was used to produce the finest plain and fancy veneers and panels.

Theodore Hanchett remained president of the company until his death in 1914. Charles Fisk, another established furniture man, replaced him. By 1915, the company had moved from the Steele Street location to a building on Allen Street Extension, which may have been the second building previously owned by Jamestown Panel Company.

By 1920, the officers of the company were Charles E. Fisk, president; N.M. Willson, general manager; T.C. Rice, secretary and treasurer; and Charles Fisk's son-in-law, Ralph G. Sage, as vice-president.

Pearl City Veneer was gone in 1924 after twenty-one years in business.

CENTURY FURNITURE CO.

Date: 1902–1910
Location: then 12–16 River Street
Founders: Charles J. Norquist and Marcus J. Norquist
Products: buffets and china closets

The Norquist name has been affiliated with furniture manufacturing in Jamestown since the 1880s. Century Furniture Company was another example of the Norquists' ventures. Established in 1902, the newly formed company officers were President Charles J. Norquist and Secretary/Treasurer Marcus J. Norquist.

Century first located at then 129 Jones Street and Gifford Avenue in a portion of the Breed-Johnson Building. The building also housed Jamestown Furniture Company, a dealer and manufacture of furniture; Eagle Foundry and machine shop; and Weber Gulick M.F.G. Company.

In 1905, Century moved to another location at then 12–16 River Street near Norquist Furniture on Chandler Street. Century's specialties were buffets and china closets.

In 1910, the building on River Street burned. The company was reorganized as Peerless Furniture Company, with the Norquist family still owning prime interest in the company.

ANCHOR FURNITURE CO.

Date: 1902–1941
Location: then 8–20 Holmes Street
Founders: Jonas E. Johnson and N. Oscar Johnson
Products: pedestal tables; telephone stands; sewing baskets; and parlor, occasional and end tables

The 1902 establishment of Anchor Furniture had Jonas E. Johnson and his brother N. Oscar Johnson as the principal owners. N. Oscar Johnson was born in Sweden in 1872 and died in 1924. He came to the United States in 1889 at the young age of seventeen, finding employment on farms in nearby Gerry and Kiantone, New York. In those early years, Oscar studied long hours to learn the English language. He completed his formal education in Randolph, New York, at the Chamberlain Institute, where he learned the cabinetmaker's trade.

Above: Anchor Furniture Company. *Jamestown, New York, Historical and Industrial Review*, 1911.

Right: N. Oscar Johnson. *History of Chautauqua County and Its People*, 1921.

In 1902, he and his brother Jonas opened a venture out of the successful Anchor Furniture Company. He was known as "NO" to his good friends and relatives.

Two other men were involved in the company for a short time: Karl Forsgren and another unidentified man. The Johnson brothers were well known in the Jamestown area for their years of experience in furniture manufacturing. They both worked at Empire Furniture and other factories in the area. Jonas was well known for his skills as a hand turner, having worked on lathes in a factory in Falconer. Jonas E. was born in Sweden in 1870 and came to Jamestown in 1893. His arrival and education very closely parallel his brother's. He died in 1933.

Anchor produced pedestals, telephone stands and sewing baskets, along with parlor, occasional and end tables, at its plant at then 8–20 Holmes Street located along the Chadakoin River, east of Institute Street. It was located in a four-story building with 21,600 square feet of floor space. The building was across from Star Furniture on the south side of Holmes Street. Anchor was equipped with the most modern devices and machinery for the production of fine furniture. Across the street from the main plant was a garage-like building that housed six turning lathes. Anchor sent its furniture to almost every state in the Union, Canada and Mexico.

The company saw a steady growth under the woodworking and business skills of the Johnson brothers. In 1902, they started the business with only five employees. By the early 1920s, they employed approximately sixty-five.

Anchor Furniture Company remained a part of the furniture scene in Jamestown for thirty-nine years and was liquidated in 1941. In 1945, a tornado blew off the top two floors of the building. That same tornado destroyed the top floors of Maddox Table Company located on Harrison Street. Artone MFG Co. now occupies the former location of the plant.

DIAMOND FURNITURE CO.

Date: 1902–1935
Location: then 46 Taylor Street
Founders: August Olson, John Love and Henry Love
Products: tables

This company was incorporated under New York State law in July 1902. Its name was changed from A.P. Olson Company to Diamond Furniture

Company at that time. The operating officers remained the same as at the former company. August P. Olson was president, John Love was vice-president and John's son Henry was secretary/treasurer. When August Olson died in 1919, John Love stayed on as vice-president until about 1923 or 1924. The business operations by that time had been turned over to Henry F. Love, and John acted as a board member and consultant for the company.

Louis Olson, the son of August, left Jamestown and relocated to Detroit. He worked as a traveling salesman representing Diamond and other furniture factories in the Jamestown area.

The factory at 46 Taylor Street operated for over sixty years, making a variety of finely crafted tables from local and imported hardwoods. The offices of the company were located at 7 Fillmore Avenue, around the corner from the Taylor Street manufacturing plant entrance. Neither of those streets exists today, having been removed by the urban renewal project of the 1970s.

The company remained in business but did not survive much past the worst years of the Depression. It was out of business in 1936. The vacant building burned on September 7, 1940.

ANDERSON VENEER DOOR CO. (JAMESTOWN VENEER CO.)

Date: 1902–1909
Location: then 111–19 Cheney Street
Founders: John S. Anderson, William Dunn, John Frew and R.C. Gailey
Products: patented Anderson Door

The groundbreaking and incorporation for this factory took place in 1902 with $100,000 in capital stock. The July 1 issue of the *Jamestown Evening Journal* has a lengthy article on the construction of this new factory located at 111–19 Cheney Street. The manufacturing structure was a three-story one-hundred- by fifty-six-foot wood frame building. An engine and boiler house, a dry kiln and several lumber sheds were planned at the time of the main factory construction. A 100-horsepower electric engine with a 125-horsepower steam boiler supplied the power for the new building.

The new company opened in 1903 with John Anderson as the proprietor. Three out-of-town investors made up the stockholders in the newly formed company. The investors were William Dunn, an undertaker from New Castle, Pennsylvania; John Frew, proprietor of the Frew Furniture Company in New Castle; and R.C. Gailey, a retired lumber dealer from New Castle. The operating officers of the organization were President John Frew, Secretary/Treasurer R.C. Gatley and General Manager John Anderson. John S. Anderson was born in 1867 and educated in Sweden. He came to America in 1887 and located in Jamestown. In 1895, Anderson joined Jamestown Sliding Blind Company, located at then 28 Briggs Street. A fire destroyed the plant in 1900. Anderson next went into business for himself, forming the J.S. Anderson Company, located at 771 East Second Street. The Anderson Company did cabinetwork, building specialty furniture, doors and some interior work. In 1902, he is listed as being one of the owners of Anderson Veneer Door Company. In September 1922, Anderson applied for a patent for a folding table and two stools that, when not in use, could be folded up to form a compact case with a handle that allowed it to be carried. He and his wife, Emma, resided at 134 Hedges Avenue.

This business venture started with the manufacture of the patented Anderson Door. From all appearances, this door looked like any other veneered door. However, the construction was different, and this solved the weak door problem. These doors did not warp, swell or come apart. The door's strength was in the wood used. Placement of the wood grain at right angles to each other greatly strengthened the door. The method of keying was also new. Several small strips inside the lock barrel allowed the key to grasp when turned, locking or unlocking the latch much like today's conventional keys. Anderson worked for eight months before he patented and was able to market the newly designed door and lock. At the outset, the new plant was to have an output of two hundred doors per day by one hundred workers.

In 1905–6, Anderson Veneer Door Company changed its name after Anderson left the business. The new company incorporated at that time under the name of Jamestown Veneer Co. The officers of the company were W.G. Dunn, president: J.M. Gardner, vice-president; J.M. Frew, treasurer; and Leonard G. Cowing, secretary and general manager. John Anderson's new company located on East Second Street manufactured veneer doors. It suffered a fire in October 1904. Jamestown Veneer Door was gone by 1909, and the location housed the F.M. Curtis Company.

F.M. Curtis Co.

Date: 1902–1922
Location: then 716–18 East Second Street
Founder: Frederick M. Curtis
Products: bedroom furniture

Founder and President Frederick M. Curtis established this company's addition to the Jamestown furniture industry in 1902. The company's first location was at 716–18 East Second Street in the Broden Table Works Building. In later years, a second location was added at 111–19 Cheney Street.

In May 1903, the company incorporated with Frederick Curtis as president and Frederick O. Crossgrove as secretary/ treasurer and general manager. Crossgrove was a businessman with many years of experience in the Jamestown furniture industry. By 1906, F.M. Curtis was still president and principal owner of the company. The company added first vice-president H.E. Curtis, a brother of Frederick. He later went on with other

The F. M. Curtis Co.

Manufacturers of Bedroom Furniture

Jamestown, New York

F.M. Curtis Co. advertisement. *Courtesy of Fenton History Center.*

Curtis family members to establish their own lumber sales yard, office and a furniture industry machine company. The second vice-president was Gust Rosenquist, and Frederick O. Crossgrove remained as the secretary/ treasurer and general manager.

In November 1908, fire destroyed the East Second Street building. Curtis moved into the other building he owned at then 111–19 Cheney Street. This second location was needed to accommodate the production of its fine line of case goods due to increased sales. This building formerly housed Standard Table and later Jamestown Veneer Company. It had about thirty thousand square feet of floor space. The employees from the burned-out building went to work in this facility. Modern machinery was installed at this plant. A private switch to the Erie Railroad tracks was located here. This enabled the company to receive rough-cut lumber and distribute finished furniture. Approximately eighty-five skilled workmen were employed at that time.

In 1911, F.M. Curtis Company produced a better grade of bedroom furniture. The shop capacity at that time was about fifty case goods (furniture) per day. The company officers were F.M. Curtis, president; S.O. Merrian, secretary/treasurer; and F.A. Rosenquist, superintendent. Frederick M. Curtis died in 1915.

In 1922, the company was known as Merrian Furniture Co., and in 1926, it became Davis Furniture Company, remaining in that location until 1956. The building on Cheney Street remains to this day.

JAMESTOWN PANEL & VENEER CO. (JAMESTOWN PANEL CO.)

Date: 1902–1993
Location: then 50 Steele Street
Founders: George Noble, Frank D. Hatch, George A. Baker and Clayton
D. Pratt
Products: veneer panels and tabletops

This company incorporated in August 1902 as Jamestown Panel and Veneer Company. The operating officers at the outset were President George Noble, Vice-president Frank D. Hatch, Secretary George A. Baker and Treasurer Clayton D. Pratt. In 1904, the company was located at then 50 Steele Street. The Finley Manufacturing Company, a small shop that produced kitchen tables, was also at this site.

From its inception, Jamestown Panel employed approximately twenty-five skilled workmen producing veneer panels, tabletops and build-up stock supplied to area furniture factories. By 1908, the president was still George Noble, but the vice-president was now A.P. Lowell.

In 1910, two large plants were in operation. The smaller of these was a two-story structure on Allen Street Extension in Falconer. It had approximately sixteen thousand square feet of floor space and was designated for the cutting of veneer sheets of every description, from mahogany to a variety of choice native woods. Approximately twenty-five workmen were employed at that location.

The main plant located at then 50 Steele Street was a three-story structure of 120 by 200 feet with about 72,000 square feet of floor space. Tabletops were manufactured here, and veneer sheets were also glued and finished at this location. The plant employed approximately 135 skilled workmen. In 1911, each plant had a private switch from the main Erie Railroad tracks. This allowed shipment of products to a wide demand of furniture manufactures throughout the country. In 1911, the officers were President D.L. Moore, Vice-president C.H. Pratt, Treasurer J.N. Chappell and Secretary L.L. Ostrander.

The company name changed around 1912, incorporating as Jamestown Panel Company. The operating officers were President Frank Morrison, Vice-president Thomas McCabe and Secretary/Treasurer Earl R. Morrison. Earl was also manager of the glued-up stock department. He worked in veneer woodworking all his business life. He was born in 1883. Upon finishing school in the Warren area, he worked for his father at Veneer and Panel Company in Warren, Pennsylvania. At the age of twenty-eight, Earl took over Salamanca Panel and Veneer Company. In 1912, young Morrison and Thomas McGabe bought up the assets of Jamestown Panel and Veneer Company. The company name was changed to Jamestown Panel Company. Morrison and McGabe also remained as directors of Warren Panel & Veneer and Salamanca Panel & Veneer Company for a number of years.

In 1919, a brick and frame addition was added, doubling the capacity of the Steele Street plant. The company was powered by electricity, with individual motors on each machine eliminating the need for belt-driven machines. By 1919, the Allen Street plant is no longer listed in the city directory. Arthur D. Patchen was also added as secretary of the company that year.

In 1920, the company operating officers were President Frank Morrison, Secretary Arthur D. Patchen and Treasurer Earl Morrison. Around 1935, the company name changed to Jamestown Veneer and Plywood Corp. Some years after, the name changed to Jamestown Plywood Company. In March 1993, the company closed its doors after ninety-one years in business.

SEABURG MANUFACTURING CO.

Date: 1903–1949
Location: then 124–30 Steele Street
Founder: Evald Seaburg
Products: parlor and library tables

This company was established in 1903 and remained part of the Jamestown furniture scene for over forty-six years. Evald Seaburg, previously a cabinetmaker at Morgan Manufacturing, purchased the old Marsh Laundry building at then 124–30 Steele Street. He renovated the four-story building for the manufacture of furniture. Evald became ill shortly after final renovations were finished and production of parlor and library tables had started. His illness was serious enough that it closed the plant for approximately four weeks. When the company reopened, ten employees and the owner worked as many as ten hours a day to fill orders. With this early success, Seaburg Manufacturing incorporated in 1905.

In 1907, two of Evald's sons joined the business. August H. Seaburg was appointed vice-president, and Ernest was appointed secretary/treasurer. The company continued to grow under Evald's supervision and skill as a cabinetmaker with a strong mechanical background. Seaburg was always looking to improve the quality of the furniture and for new products to expand his line. Some of those items added were cedar chests and medicine and shaving cabinets. A very unique and exclusive product was the LIBROLA, a phonograph in a library table.

In 1912, two more sons became of age and joined the family business. Oscar and Victor were listed as being employed but did not hold positions as officers until 1914. At that time, Oscar was listed as assistant secretary and Victor was listed as secretary in the Jamestown City Directory.

By 1914, the company had grown to a forty-man workforce in a building with 25,000 square feet of floor space. This substantial growth made it necessary to add buildings in 1914 and again in 1920. One of the buildings in 1920 was a three-story 110- by 21-foot reinforced concrete building. The ground floor was a modern dry kiln, and the upper floors were lumber storage areas. The dry lumber moved from the kiln on the first floor to a seven-ton elevator that raised the bundles of lumber to the top two stories for storage. This was the only three-story dry kiln in the country that used this type of handling practice.

The continued growth of the company in 1920 increased staff to seventy-five employees. The officers were listed in the city directory as President August Seaburg, Vice-president Victor Seaburg, Secretary Oscar Seaburg and Treasurer and General Manager Ernest Seaburg. Evald turned the company over to his four sons around 1921 and retired to his home on Catlin Avenue in Jamestown. Evald was born in Sweden. He apprenticed as a young man to a cabinetmaker. He later owned a plant that manufactured threshing machines. He built all the parts for the machines, thereby cutting the expense of purchasing original and replacement parts. He married Johanna Hanson a few months after his twenty-first birthday, coming to the United States in 1891. He used his cabinetmaking skills at Morgan Manufacturing Company, remaining there for eleven years and working his way up to superintendent. In 1903, he resigned and, with his sons, started Seaburg Manufacturing Company. He was active in the Swedish community and was one of the founders of the First Lutheran Church in Jamestown. Evald died in 1926, and his wife died in 1934.

His son August died in December 1939 at the age of fifty-three. Oscar died in March 1954. Victor left the family firm in 1930. He became the Chicago sales manager for Jamestown Lounge Company and died in 1969 at age eighty-one.

The company was noted for keeping up with the latest improvements in machinery and equipment. Evald was always the innovator of new and better processing practices even after his retirement from the day-to-day operations. One of the first major improvements was the timesaving use of spray guns rather than brush-wielding specialists for varnishing. By the mid-1920s, Seaburg Manufacturing was regarded as one of the most modern of any Jamestown furniture factory.

In 1927, Espey Upholstery occupied part of the Seaburg building on Steele Street. Seaburg may have leased some of the building to it.

By 1948, Seaburg was out of the Steele Street building, with its location listed as 250 Crescent Street. By 1949, no listing for Seaburg is recorded in the city directory. A portion of the company's interest may have been purchased by Union National, another local furniture manufacture. The Jamestown Light Plant offices now occupy the land where the buildings were located.

NELSON & CO.

Date: 1903–1920
Location: behind H.P. Robertson on Steele Street
Founders: Lars A. Larson and Gust A. Nelson
Product: dining tables

This company first shows up in the 1903 city directory. The shop owners were affiliated with Nelson, Bergland & Company, established around 1893 and located at 10–22 Steele Street behind Jamestown Bedstead. New operating officer Lars A. Larson and one of the founding officers of Nelson, Bergland, Gust A. Nelson, established this company.

The small shop was located at then 40–48 Steele Street behind H.P. Robertson Company in a large building connected by an overhead walkway. The location of both these shops is near the former Evans roller-skating building. The small company produced a variety of dining tables. In 1920, the Stratton Furniture Company incorporated and took over Nelson & Company. In 1932, Tillotson furniture is listed in that location.

MUNSON & JOHNSON CO.

Date: 1903–1914
Location: then 710–12 East Second and Winsor Streets
Founders: Charles F. Munson and Fred J. Johnson
Products: wood mantels

Charles F. Munson and Fred J. Johnson established this company in 1903 in the Munson & Waite Building located then at 710–12 East Second and Winsor Streets. They produced a wide variety of wood mantels for the furniture industry. In 1908, a fire destroyed the F.M. Curtis factory at 716–18 East Second Street. Portions of the Munson & Johnson factory were also damaged in the fire. However, the business was saved and continued at that location until about 1914. Monarch Furniture Company occupied the building in 1915.

LIBERTY FURNITURE CO.

Date: 1904–1909
Location: then 11–15 Blackstone Avenue
Founders: Frank P. and Charles M. Johnson
Products: dressers, dressing tables and chiffoniers

The groundbreaking for the new building and the newly formed Liberty Furniture Company was on Thursday, September 24, 1903. The new plant was a four-story brick building 50 by 130 feet in size. A 30- by 33-foot boiler and engine house was planned. Two 37- by 46-foot dry kilns were built with the capacity to dry 60,000 feet of lumber at once. The owners of the plant estimated at least seventy-six employees occupied the new buildings. About thirty-five people were employed at the outset.

Liberty incorporated in July 1904. The president was Frank P. Johnson, and the vice-president was his brother, Charles M. Johnson. The Johnsons were previously employed at Empire Furniture. Liberty produced a line of dressers, chiffoniers and dressing tables. The plant was located at then 11–15 Blackstone Avenue next to the Dahlstrom complex. In 1906, L. Clyde Stewart was listed as the secretary/treasurer. The company's last year in business was 1909, when it was bought out by Atlas Furniture Company.

BAILEY TABLE CO.

Date: 1904–1931
Location: Harrison, Winsor and Willard Streets (old Breed Buildings)
Founders: Clayton E. and Benjamin M. Bailey
Products: tables

The Bailey Table Company originated as a small table shop with roots in Silver Creek, New York. The company began the manufacture of marble-top tables in the 1870s under the ownership of Beman P. Sold. It relocated to Jamestown in the early 1880s and continued production of marble-top tables under the name of Beman, Breed & Phillips. The directors and officers of the company were J.M. Beman, Charles Breed and Hurley L. Phillips.

In 1885, the company name and principal owners changed to Phillips, Maddox Company. After only a year, the name and owners became Morgan, Maddox and then Maddox, Bailey in 1890, and again in 1898 the name would change to Bailey-Jones Company. In 1904, the company became Bailey Table. It incorporated in 1911. The officers were Clayton E. Bailey, president, and Benjamin M. Bailey, vice-president.

In 1913, the president was Benjamin M. Bailey and vice-president was Charles W. Herrick. David W. Schench was secretary, and Carl L. Liedblad was treasurer and superintendent.

The company occupied two large buildings, one on Harrison and Winsor and one on Willard Street. One building was six stories high and the other five stories high, and they were connected by an overhead passageway that crossed Winsor Street. There were dry kilns and lumber storage buildings next to the Willard Street facility. The two large buildings were formerly part of Breed Furniture, the first water-powered furniture factory in Jamestown.

Bailey produced parlor tables, library tables and dining room suites. It employed approximately three hundred workers at peak production and was one of the largest Jamestown furniture employers.

The Bailey plant failed and was out of business sometime in 1930. Web Machine used one of the buildings. Some years later, the buildings were razed, and nothing remains today.

FOUR DISTINCT TYPES OF WOOD FURNITURE MANUFACTURING

When owners organized furniture shops, they chose from four distinct types of manufacturing styles:

1. A manufacturer owning timber properties. Most manufactures felt that ownership of timberland was not economical. Logging and sawmills are best run as separate operations.

2. A manufacturer purchases rough-cut lumber from wholesalers. Upon receipt of this lumber, the furniture manufacture stores it for air-drying It is next kiln dried, slashed into desired sizes, glued, cut to dimension, machined and assembled into furniture. The finish is applied as a final process. The veneering of furniture will fall into this most popular form of manufacturing furniture.

3. The manufacturer buys the dimension stock and does the machining, assembles and applies the final finish to the completed furniture.

4. A manufacturer buys various ready-to-assemble parts and applies the final finish to the furniture.

The third and fourth types were not considered best economically and were used by only a small percentage of the furniture manufacturers.

LEVEL FURNITURE CO.

Date: 1904–1929
Location: Allen Street Extension
Founders: Gust C. Peterson, William Bjork, John M. Anderson and Frank
O. Ruckman
Products: library and parlor tables, phonograph cabinets

Gust C. Peterson and a group of investors established this furniture company in 1904. Initially, he intended to manufacture library and parlor tables exclusively. That viewpoint changed, and other furniture commodities were added. One of the most successful lines was the phonograph cabinet.

The plant was established on Allen Street Extension in the current location of Bush Industries next to Crawford Furniture (Atlas Furniture). Initially, samples for the new line of furniture were made in the old Martyn Building on Fourth Street.

Gust C. Peterson was born in 1874 in Jamestown. He went to work at a very early age to help support his family. He worked for a short period of time at Jamestown Worsted Mills and then at Broadhead Mills. Child labor laws required Peterson to leave the factory and attend school. At the age of fourteen, he returned to the workforce, finding employment at Newman's Spring Bed Factory. He then went to Breed & Johnson Company, where he was a machine hand. He moved to Fenton Roberts Sideboard Company in Falconer, New York. He returned to Breed & Johnson after the company reorganized. As a young man, Peterson acquired excellent woodworking skills while continuing his education at the night school in Jamestown. Peterson continued his employment at Maddox Table Company as a sample builder. By this time, others in the furniture business were noticing his skills. He joined Bailey Jones Company, securing a management position, increasing his salary and gaining knowledge about the business side of furniture factories. In 1904, he and others in the furniture business united in establishing the Level Furniture Company. His position was general manager and a director of the company.

In 1905, Level was incorporated. The operating officers were William Bjork, president; John M. Anderson, vice-president; and Frank O. Ruckman, secretary/treasurer. The directors were A. Carlson, Oscar Bloomquist, George V. Olson and Elmer Jones. Gust C. Peterson was manager and chairman of the board. In 1904, this company employed thirty skilled workmen. The factory floor spanned ten thousand square feet, with space for expansion.

By 1911, this successful company was found in a three-story building 70 by 115 feet with approximately 24,000 square feet of floor space. The shop was equipped with the most modern machinery for the manufacture of parlor and library tables in fine exotic and domestic woods. Throughout the plant, fifty-five skilled workers built the furniture in several departments.

By 1920, the company had expanded to a workforce of 275 with seventy-five thousand square feet of floor space. Most of the time, this area was congested with finished furniture waiting to be shipped. This bottleneck was due in part to the manufacture and sale of phonograph cabinets mainly for the Edison Phonograph Machine Company. The plant was always equipped with the latest in woodworking machines, and Level's products were always of the highest grade. A 175-horsepower steam engine and a 75-horsepower electric engine powered the plant.

The officers of the company were John M. Anderson, president; Joseph Bloomquist, secretary/treasurer; and Gust C. Peterson, manager. Joseph A. Bloomquist was born in 1886 in Portland, New York. As a youngster, he was sent to live with his aunt on her farm in Minnesota. He attended grammar and high school there. Upon his return to Jamestown, he entered Jamestown Business College, taking a two-year course in business training and office practice. In 1903, he was employed by the Jamestown Lounge Company as a clerk, remaining there four years. He then took on the bookkeeper position at Level Furniture Company. In only two years, he was admitted as a partner and made secretary/treasurer of the company.

The company lasted only nine years longer and failed in 1929.

GOLDEN FURNITURE CO.

Date: 1904–1912
Location: Martyn Building on Fourth Street
Founders: Charles Caster, Frank O. Anderson and Hjalmer C. Lindros
Products: dressers and chiffoniers

This addition to the Jamestown-area furniture industry was incorporated in November 1904 with a capital stock of $10,000 and Charles Caster as president, Frank O. Anderson as vice-president and Hjalmer C. Lindros as secretary. Karl Forsgren was involved initially, staying a short time before moving to Warren, Pennsylvania, to start a company there. Golden Furniture

Golden Furniture Company. *Jamestown, New York, Historical and Industrial Review*, 1911.

Golden Furniture office. *Courtesy of Fenton History Center.*

Golden Furniture cabinet room. *Courtesy of Fenton History Center.*

Golden Furniture packing room. *Courtesy of Fenton History Center.*

was located in one of Martyn Furniture's frame buildings on Fourth Street, manufacturing dressers and chiffoniers (a narrow, high chest of drawers, sometimes with a mirror attached).

Golden Furniture finishing room. *Courtesy of Fenton History Center.*

The company suffered a fire in July 1906 but recovered and relocated to a brick building on Fifth and Clinton Streets with Martyn Furniture. By 1911, Golden employed approximately seventy workmen at the plant and twelve traveling salesmen. By that time, it had expanded to the building of Excelsior Furniture Company, located at 151 Jones and Gifford Avenue, close to the Erie Railroad tracks. The building had about forty thousand square feet of floor space.

Fire occurred two times in May 1911, destroying the two top floors. The company rebuilt these two floors both times. The last listing in the city directory is in 1912.

MARVEL FURNITURE CO.

Date: 1904–1932
Location: West Eighth Street
Founders: Alfred A. Anderson and Warner F. Liedblad
Products: bedroom furniture

Above: Marvel Furniture Company. *Jamestown, New York, Historical and Industrial Review*, 1911.

Left: Oscar E. Anderson. *History of Chautauqua County and Its People*, 1921.

Marvel Furniture was established in 1904. Alfred A. Anderson was president and general manager, his brother Oscar was vice-president and the secretary/treasurer was Warner F. Liedblad. These men had extensive experience in the furniture industry. They took an active interest in the progress and development of their business and the Jamestown community.

Oscar E. Anderson was born in Sweden in October 1880. He was educated in Sweden until the age of twelve, when he began working on the family farm. At age fifteen, he immigrated to the United States to live with relatives in Jamestown. In 1895, he began work at Empire Furniture Company. He later moved on to Marvel Furniture, working days, and attended night school to learn the English language and business management. He was promoted to sales representative for Marvel and other Jamestown furniture companies. He entered into business with Marcus J. Norquist in 1919 and founded Monarch Furniture. Some years later, he became vice-president, treasurer and general manager of Dahlstrom Metallic Door Company. Still later, he was associated with Jamestown Metal Desk Company (Jamestown Metal Corp.). Oscar died in November 1937 at his Foote Avenue home.

Warner Liedblad was born in Sweden in 1863. He came to the United States with his parents at the age of four. When he became of age, he went to work for Empire Furniture Company. He worked his way up through the company and was promoted to superintendent of the finishing department. In 1907, he joined Alfred and Oscar Anderson in establishing Marvel Furniture. He remained with the company until it was liquidated in 1932. He died in October 1942 at the age of seventy-nine.

Alfred A. Anderson was born in Sweden in 1876. He came to Jamestown in 1892 at the age of sixteen. He worked at A.C. Norquist Company, quickly learning the cabinetmaking trade. He went on to work with his brother Frank, the founder of Empire Furniture Company. In 1904, he organized Marvel Furniture, and in 1917, Alfred and Oscar were officers at Monarch. Alfred died unexpectedly at age sixty in 1936.

Initially, Marvel Furniture produced a high-grade line of bedroom furniture in a building that formerly housed the C.C. Wilson planing mill located on West Eighth Street. Marvel started small, with only 2 employees plus Anderson and Liedblad. In 1907, the company incorporated and moved into a five-story structure with sixty-five thousand square feet of floor space located at then 1077 Allen Street. This new plant was equipped with the most modern machinery and appliances for the manufacture of fine bedroom furniture, including but not limited to dressers, chiffoniers and washstands. In 1911, Marvel held steady employment for

Marvel Furniture Company. *Courtesy of Fenton History Center.*

Marvel Furniture Company. *Courtesy of Fenton History Center.*

approximately 125 workers. Its extensive line of products was marketed throughout the United States.

This company remained in business for over twenty-five years and was liquidated in 1932.

The Grandeur of a Plant Name

A flamboyant name and manner for the furniture factories was an important ingredient for the spirit of the day. This was reflected in names like Marvel, Empire, Union, Monarch, National, Elite, Atlas, Diamond and Superior.

H.P. Robertson Co.

Date: 1905–1931
Location: Steele Street (near skating rink)
Founder: Henry P. Robertson
Products: tables and folding beds

Incorporated in 1905, the former company was the long-established Jamestown Bedstead Company. Henry P. Robertson was the president and treasurer of the newly formed company. Charles Ipson, a longtime employee of Jamestown Bedstead, was vice-president. John Ipson, Charles's son, was secretary. The newly formed company manufactured tables and folding beds at its Steele Street location.

In 1906, Anchor Furniture Company shared the building. In 1907, the company moved to a building on Holmes Street.

John H. Ipson. *Illustrated History of Jamestown,* 1900.

Robertson was gone by 1931. Tillotson Furniture occupied the building in 1932 and remained until 1959 or 1960.

ECKMAN FURNITURE CO.

Date: 1905–1927
Location: then 129 Jones and Gifford Avenue
Founders: John and Charles Eckman
Products: desks, dining and bedroom furniture, bookcases, buffets and china cabinets

Established in 1905, Eckman Furniture, formerly Breed-Johnson Company, did not change its name until approximately 1912. The owners of this newly formed company were John and Charles Eckman.

The Eckman brothers had been employed by Breed-Johnson Company since about 1894. Charles was the secretary/treasurer and general manager. John was the president and remained in that position.

The company was located at then 129 Jones and Gifford Avenue in a three-story brick building. In 1912, the product line included fancy desks, dining room and bedroom furniture, bookcases, buffets and

Eckman Furniture Co.

Fancy Desks, Book Cases
Buffets, China Cabinets
and Other Cabinet Ware

JAMESTOWN, NEW YORK

C. L. ECKMAN, Secretary, Treasurer and Manager

Eckman Furniture Co. advertisement.
Courtesy of Fenton History Center.

china cabinets. The company had its own siding connecting with the main line of the Erie Railroad.

Eckman Furniture was out of business by 1927. Randolph Furniture Works purchased the interest of the Eckman plant and remained in business until 1955. In 1957, the Art Metal Corporation expanded and took over the empty building.

The Eckmans' father, Nels, was a foreman in the refinery department of Standard Oil Company. He was such a skillful workman that the company sent him to Buffalo to assist in the construction of a refinery there. In later years, he worked for his sons as an engineer in the furniture factory. John was born in 1868 in Sweden and came to Titusville, Pennsylvania, with the family in 1869. He received his education at the grammar and high schools in Titusville. John began his business career at Standard Oil in Titusville, obtaining employment in the same department as his father. He remained there for three years before going to work for a furniture manufacture in Titusville. John and his brother Charles went to work at Breed-Johnson Furniture in about 1894 and became owners of the company in 1905.

In 1920, John and others formed Jamestown Metal Desk, seeing the changing market from wooden commercial office furniture to metal. John became president of that company. He was very musically inclined and owned a music store located on the fifth floor of the Wellman Building on West Third Street. John died at the age of seventy-seven in 1945.

Charles L. Eckman was born in Sweden in 1866. When he was only three, the family came to Titusville, Pennsylvania. He was educated in the public schools of Titusville. Upon completion of his education, he worked as a clerk at the Commercial Bank of Titusville. Sometime after, he was an accountant at S.S. Bryan & Company in Titusville. Charles moved to Buffalo, where he studied telegraph. In 1894, he arrived in Jamestown and went to work for Breed-Johnson Furniture Company. He advanced to secretary of the company and was later promoted to treasurer and general manager. In 1905, he and his brother bought the business. Charles died at the age of eighty-four in 1950.

ALLIANCE FURNITURE

Date: 1905–1952
Location: then 611–15 Allen Street
Founders: Edward Bergquist, Gustaf A. Lund, Charles Berglund, August A. Sandberg, Oscar Carlson and Joseph Carlson
Products: dining room furniture

This company was incorporated on January 5, 1905. Eight men pooled their resources and formed Alliance Furniture. Among the founders were the operating officers of the company: Edward Bergquist, Gustaf A. Lund, Charles Berglund, August A. Sandberg, Oscar Carlson and Joseph Carlson. In 1905 and 1906, Charles Berglund was president, Oscar Carlson was secretary/treasurer and superintendent of the newly formed company was Edward Bergquist.

Alliance produced a better grade of dining room furniture in a wide variety of attractive designs from the choicest oaks and mahogany. It did not take long before its original establishment became inadequate due to the phenomenal growth of the business. A location at then 611–15 Allen Street was purchased, and a three-story building, 48 by 56 feet, was erected. The original wood frame building was replaced by a four-story building, 64 by 152 feet, with 27,000 square feet of floor space. The new building was equipped with the latest mechanical woodworking devices. The company continued to prosper, producing fine-quality dining room furniture as its specialty.

By 1911, the company supplied steady work for about fifty skilled men, marketing its product throughout the eastern United States. The officers were Gustaf A. Lund, president; August Sandberg, vice-president; A.E. Eckberg, secretary/treasurer; and Edward Bergquist, superintendent.

Charles W. Berglund was born in 1871 in Sweden. He came with his parents to the United States at the age of three. He attended the local public schools until the age of eleven, when he went to work. He was employed by the A.C. Norquist Company. While there, he learned band sawing and gained competent knowledge of other branches of the furniture business. He worked hard at his trade, spending long hours at home continuing his labors. His lack of education did not stop him from obtaining a better command of the English language and knowledge of business requirements. In 1905, he and other furniture investors organized the Alliance Furniture Company. Berglund died at the young age of thirty-four in July 1905. Upon his death, his wife, Elizabeth, retained his interest in the company.

Edward Bergquist was born in Sweden in 1867, one of six sons. His father, Andrew, was a coffin maker in Smoland. Edward had three years of schooling in Sweden before the family came to Jamestown in 1876. He went to work at the age of fifteen for a novelty manufacturing company located on Willard Street. Looking to better himself, he went to work in Buffalo for Jewel Refrigerator, a company that produced iceboxes. While there, he married and returned to Jamestown with his wife, Eva (Lindberg) Bergquist, around 1892. He worked at a number of furniture factories, including Union Furniture, before he and seven others would band together and form Alliance Furniture in 1905. Bergquist became superintendent and remained in that position until ill health forced him to retire in 1917. He died in September 1918 at the age of fifty-one.

Gustaf A. Lund was born in Sweden in 1875 and came to Jamestown alone when he was only seventeen years old. He continued his education in Jamestown, working days and going to night school. He entered the woodworking factories and learned the cabinetmaking trade, as well as the business of building furniture. One of the local companies he worked for was Jamestown Bedstead Company. He eventually grouped with other residents of the Swedish community to establish Alliance Furniture. By 1920, Lund was the president of the company. Like other business owners of the day, he did not hesitate to soil his hands when there was a need. The employees recognized his excellent expertise in the knowledge of cabinetmaking. In times when a deadline loomed, he was called to work with the other cabinetmakers in the shop. He died in August 1957 at the age of eighty-two.

By 1920, the operating officers of the company were Gustaf A. Lund, president and superintendent; Oscar Carlson, vice-president and director; August Sandberg, director; Axel Eckberg, secretary/treasurer; and Joseph Carlson and Hjalmar Sandberg, directors. The building on Allen Street burned in 1952.

In 1956, the Allen Street land was cleared, making room for new offices and a warehouse for Proto Tool Company (formerly Plomb Tool Company).

NATIONAL FURNITURE CO.

Date: 1905–1940
Location: then 501–03 West Fourth Street (Martyn Building)
Founders: Carl I. Johnson, Charles P. Sandberg and Ray Anderson
Products: parlor and library tables

Incorporated in 1905, National's first location was at then 501–03 West Fourth Street, in the Martyn Furniture Building. The president of the company was Carl I. Johnson, the vice-president was Charles P. Sandberg and the secretary/treasurer was Ray Anderson. It first produced fine parlor and library tables and later changed its line to bedroom furniture. In 1906, a fire broke out at the Fourth Street location, prompting the company to move. In 1908, it moved to a building at then 150 Blackstone Avenue.

By 1912, the officers were President and Superintendent Carl I. Johnson, Secretary John A. Nord and Treasurer Axel Peterson. The last city directory listing was 1938. In 1939, the Blackstone Avenue plant was vacant. The building became part of Watson Manufacturing Co. in about 1941. National Furniture merged with Union Furniture in 1940, becoming Union National, located at 234 Crescent Street. The connection with respect to the merger of the companies was Carl I. Johnson. He was married to Augusta Nord, sister of the founders of Union Furniture.

JAMESTOWN TABLE CO.

Date: 1906–1962
Location: then 145–53 Fairmount Avenue
Founders: Cyrus E. Jones and Lewis C. Jagger
Products: parlor and library tables

This Jamestown furniture company was established in 1906 with capital stock holdings of $60,000. The original company was Morgan Manufacturing, founded in 1890. The new company founders were Cyrus E. Jones and one of the Morgan Company investors, Lewis C. Jagger. The company manufactured a variety of parlor and library tables.

The building was located at then 145–53 Fairmount Avenue, close to the Fairmount Avenue Bridge. The street was known as Ashville Avenue until about 1908. In 1906, the operating officers were President Lewis C. Jagger, Vice-president Charles I. Moore, Secretary Thomas E. Perkins and Treasurer Richard Peart. The chairman of the board was the well-known investor Cyrus E. Jones.

Changes within the operating officers of the company began in 1913. The new officers were President Charles Moore, Vice-president Thomas Perkins and Secretary/Treasurer Richard Peart.

In 1913, Jagger and other members of the firm acquired investment interest in the company, and Peart sold out in 1915. Ralph Taylor bought out the interest of Charles I. Moore in May 1917, becoming president of the corporation. That same year, the company began producing bedroom furniture and discontinued its line of tables. By 1920, the Jamestown Table

Company officers were President Ralph W. Taylor, Vice-president Thomas E. Perkins and Secretary/Treasurer James Tillotson Jr. The company became Taylor Jamestown in 1962, with Ralph Taylor and his son as president and vice-president. In 1965, the plant on Fairmount Avenue burned.

James Tillotson came from Grand Rapids, Michigan, and joined Jamestown Table in 1906 as a stockholder. In 1916 or 1917, Tillotson became the secretary/treasurer of the company. He bought out H.P. Robertson Company and changed the name to Tillotson Furniture Company, locating on Steele Street.

Cyrus E. Jones was a capitalist who had been investing in the furniture industry in Jamestown since before 1890. He was born in Ellicott in 1863, the son of a minister. Upon completion of his schooling, he moved to New York City. He took a position as a manufacturer and importer of fancy goods. He returned to Jamestown after seventeen years to work for C.E. Bailey. Jones was active in many city affairs. He was one of the founders of the Jamestown Manufactures Association and president of the Jamestown Post Publishing Company. Jones died on October 13, 1922, at the age of fifty-nine.

Ralph W. Taylor was born in November 1883. He was educated in the Jamestown public schools and attended Jamestown Business College. His business career began with L.C. and L.E. Railroad. In 1905, he accepted a position with Bailey Jones Company as secretary/treasurer. In 1917, he joined Jamestown Table Company.

JAMESTOWN CHAIR CO.

Date: 1906–1932
Location: then 20 Winsor Street (near Jamestown Lounge)
Founders: S.P. Carlson, Charles E. Jones and Charles W. Swanson
Products: rockers and dining room chairs

The large plant established in 1906 as Jamestown Chair Company was formerly the Y.W. Burtch & Company, a manufacturer of chairs established in 1880. The founders of the new company were S.P. Carlson, Charles E. Jones and Charles W. Swanson. From the outset, it produced a high-grade line of rockers and dining room chairs in a wide variety of attractive designs, using the choicest woods. The factory was located next to the Jamestown Lounge Company, at then 20 Winsor Street, in a four-story building with sixteen thousand square feet of floor space. The structure was equipped with the latest machinery and appliances.

Throughout its history, the company operated on the principle that each workman should be trained to do a specific job. This early production line system of manufacturing seems to have produced a better article of furniture. With this system, the consumer received a product superior in materials and workmanship—a better chair at a lesser price. This resulted in increased sales and profits. Workers also benefited, since they were rewarded with better wages. In 1911, approximately thirty full-time workmen were given steady employment in the various departments. Their product found a ready market throughout the United States, while a considerable export trade with South America was maintained. Some Jamestown Chair Company chairs were sold as part of dining room sets made by other local companies, such as Alliance Furniture and Union Furniture.

The company also benefited from the leadership of its managing officers, who were first- and second-generation Swedish immigrants. Charles E. Jones, one of the three company founders, was born in Sweden in 1865. After coming to Jamestown in 1888, he found work as a cabinetmaker for Ahlstrom Piano Company. He eventually served Jamestown Chair Company in the role of superintendent, a position he held until his death in April 1917 at the age of fifty-two.

Another one of the company founders, Charles W. Swanson, was born in Smoland, Sweden, in 1870. When he was only a year old, his parents relocated to the United States and settled in Jamestown. As a teenager, he worked as a delivery boy for the New York Tea Store. He also worked for two weeks at Y.W. Burtch & Company in the sanding department. The furniture business was not in his immediate future. He soon began clerking at the J.F. Peterson Shoe Store. In 1893, he opened a shoe store at 3 South Main Street. He and his brother-in-law, Elim E. Holmberg, incorporated the business under the name of Swanson-Holmberg Shoe Company in 1912. Holmberg became the general manager. After Swanson helped establish the Jamestown Chair Company, the same brother-in-law eventually followed him into the furniture business. The new venture was hardly foreign to Holmberg. Born in Jamestown in 1881, Elim E. Holmberg was the son of Gustave Holmberg, one of the founders of the Swedish Furniture Company (Atlas). As a young man, Elim worked for his father for three years in the packing and shipping department of Atlas Furniture.

When the Jamestown Chair Company reorganized in 1920, Charles W. Swanson moved from the role of secretary/treasurer (a position he had held since 1910) and assumed the responsibilities of president and general manager. Elim Holmberg became the secretary, and Peter E. Larson became vice-president. S.G. Jacobson, who had been with the company as office bookkeeper since 1910, took the position of treasurer.

The company remained in business another dozen years before dissolving in 1932. The building was razed sometime after the closing, eventually making way for the parking lot that is located on the site today. Swanson died in 1934, after a number of prosperous years in Jamestown. His brother-in-law, Elim E. Holmberg, passed away in March 1943 at the age of sixty-two.

AMERICAN CARVING WORKS

Date: 1906–1928
Location: 516 West Fourth Street (Martyn Brothers Building)
Founders: Adolf C. Schulze, Jacob Van Stee and Rudolph Schulze
Products: bedroom tables, telephone stands, pedestals, tabourets and woodcarving on table pedestals

Adolf C. Schulze, Jacob Van Stee and Rudolph Schulze established this company in 1906. The company had previously been established as Jamestown Art Carving Works with Jacob Van Stee as the founder. This company produced a fine array of bedroom tables, telephone stands, pedestals, tabourets and woodcarving on table pedestals. Its specialty was the patented manufacturing of a folding table. That table was a popular export item, with a number of them going to Australia.

The company was first located in the Martyn Building and then moved to 34 Taylor Street. A new building was constructed in 1912 at 200 Crescent Street to accommodate the growing business. It was a three-story structure with seven thousand square feet of floor space. In 1912, American employed approximately twenty skilled workmen. In 1916, Van Stee disposed of his holdings and established Schulze & Van Stee. In 1928, the business was sold, and two years later, it became known as Alder, Van Stee Corporation. In 1933, the business became Van Stee Corporation when the Alders disposed of their holdings to Van Stee.

EAGLE FURNITURE CO.

Date: 1907–1920
Location: then 61 Water Street
Founders: John G. Hallstrom and C. Herman Erickson
Products: pedestals and tabourets

This company incorporated in 1907, employing approximately twenty-five skilled workmen. John G. Hallstrom was president and C. Herman Erickson was secretary/treasurer of the company. Eagle Furniture was located in a two-story, five-thousand-square-foot building constructed of sheet iron at then 61 Water Street. Eagle manufactured an exclusive line of high-grade pedestals and tabourets in a wide variety of designs from the choicest mahogany and native woods. In 1912, the operating officers of Eagle were President Carl A. Lundquist, Vice-president C.G. Telt and secretary/treasurer C. Herman Erickson. Lundquist became one of the owners of C.A. Lundquist & Company, a hardware and tinsmith business located in Brooklyn Square.

By 1920, Eagle was no longer in business. Premier Cabinet Company occupied the Water Street building. In 1937–38, Maddox Table made radio cabinets. In 1940, Burns Case Goods Corp. manufactured from the Water Street location. The Eagle Furniture building no longer exists, and W.C.A. Hospital occupies the approximate location on Water Street.

CHADAKOIN FURNITURE CO.

Date: 1907–1913
Location: then 100 Steele Street
Founders: Frank D. Hatch, Charles W. Eckman, Edmund S. Smith and Wrothwell Butterfield
Products: parlor and library tables

This company first appears in the 1907 Jamestown City Directory, listed as manufacturing woven wire mattresses and steel springs. In 1909, the company relocated to then 100 Steel Street. It was listed as a manufacture of parlor and library tables. The president of the company was Frank D. Hatch, vice-president was Charles W. Eckman, secretary was Edmund S. Smith and treasurer was Wrothwell Butterfield. By 1913, the company was gone and Jamestown Carving and Manufacturing was listed at the Steele Street location.

Banner Furniture

Date: 1907–1913
Location: 84–92 Steele Street
Founder: Paul Rosencrantz
Products: dressers and chiffoniers

This shop was gone by 1913 but, while in business, expanded its product line to include chamber and dining room furniture. In 1909–10, the vice-president and superintendent was Gustaf Olson and the secretary/treasurer was W.S. Bailey. It suffered a loss at the Grand Rapids, Michigan Furniture Exposition when fire destroyed its exhibits stored in a building there. In 1913, H.H. Roberts occupied that location. He was a jobber (salesman) dealing in mahogany lumber and veneers.

Jamestown Cabinet Co.

Date: 1908–1920?
Location: then 771 East Second Street
Founders: Frank G. Curtis and Oscar Pang
Products: dressers, chiffoniers and dressing tables

This shop was established in 1908 in a building that previously housed the J.S. Anderson Company at then 771 East Second Street. In 1909, Frank G. Curtis was president and Oscar Pang was secretary/treasurer. Frank remained as president for approximately one year. His brother Frederick took over as president in 1911. Frederick M. Curtis owned F.M. Curtis Company, established in 1902. In 1911, Oscar E. Anderson was vice-president and treasurer. He became one of the founders of Monarch Furniture in 1914. Oscar R. Pang remained as secretary through the duration of the company. The company manufactured dressers, chiffoniers and dressing tables in quartered oak, mahogany, walnut and Birdseye maple. Its superior line of phonograph cabinets was made with the best mahoganies. Machinery and appliances used in the manufacturing of furniture were of the latest developments. It employed twenty-five workers in 1911 and was located in a large two-story building with a basement. In 1916, the company is listed as Jamestown Cabinet Company (Inc.). The officers were Cheston Price, president and treasurer; Oscar R. Pang, secretary and assistant treasurer; and Joseph J. Carlson, general manager. The building on Second Street was vacant by 1920.

SUPERIOR FURNITURE CO.

Date: 1908–1938
Location: then 167 Jones and Gifford Avenue
Founders: Frank O. Norquist and Austin E. Anderson
Products: dining and extension tables

This company was established in 1908, when longtime furniture men from the Jamestown area pooled their resources to manufacture extension tables. The company was incorporated with capital stock holdings of $10,000. Frank O. Norquist, Austin E. Anderson and four other investors purchased the bankrupted Johnson Table Company at then 167 Jones and Gifford Avenue. The building was a two-story structure of approximately ten thousand square feet equipped with every machine for the manufacture of fine dining and extension tables. In 1910, Norquist and Anderson bought out the other four investors and became the principal officers and owners of the company. In 1911, the company supplied steady work for a skilled workforce of thirty men. Its product was shipped throughout the United States.

In 1920, the officers of the company were President Frank O. Norquist, Vice-president Austin E. Anderson and Secretary/Treasurer Marvin Anderson. Austin's father, Charles E. Anderson, was brought in as superintendent of the plant. Reynold Norquist was an assistant under his father, Frank.

This company went through an astounding growth period, going from $13,000 worth of furniture shipped at the outset to $140,000 worth of chairs shipped in 1918. A large addition was added to the Jones and Gifford plant to accommodate the increased production. The owners realized early on the growth potential and larger profit yields in manufacturing just chairs. They discontinued the other lines to concentrate on that venture, which paid off nicely. The last listing for this company was 1938; the building was vacant in 1939.

Austin E. Anderson came from humble circumstances. He was born in Jamestown in 1888. His father had worked in furniture factories since coming to this country and earned a humble living. His mother, Minnie, died when Austin was only seven years old. He attended public schools and, while in his last two years of high school, found congenial employment as assistant secretary at the Jamestown YMCA. After graduation and for one year following, he continued as secretary for the boys' department of the local YMCA. He then went to work as a clerk at the Erie Railroad Company freight house. In 1906, he became a bookkeeper at Johnson Table Company, thinking it would offer him an opportunity for advancement. The company filed for bankruptcy four months after Anderson arrived. He then went into a partnership with Frank O. Norquist and four others. This venture became the founding of Superior Furniture Company. In December 1970, Austin Anderson died at age eighty-two.

Frank O. Norquist was born in Sweden in 1866. His family came to America when he was only three years old. They settled in Jamestown, and young Frank attended public schools in Jamestown. His family purchased a farm in Lander, Pennsylvania. Frank started to attend school there, but after only a few years, the Norquist family sold the farm and moved back to Jamestown. Frank attended the Jamestown public schools until the age of fifteen. He went to work at Broadhead Mills for one year and then took a clerical position at Allen's Auction House for two years. He went on to work for his brother August at A.C. Norquist located on Chandler Street in Jamestown. He held the position of clerk and bookkeeper there for three years. At the end of that period, Frank was promoted and became a partner, holding the position of secretary and treasurer of the newly reorganized Norquist Brothers. During this time, he was one of the founders of a retail furniture business and a founder of Union Furniture Company on Crescent Street. In 1907, Frank became president of Superior Furniture. In 1918, his brother August bought out his interest in Norquist Brothers. In 1919, he founded Allied Furniture Company with partner Austin E. Anderson. Frank Norquist died in August 1938 at age seventy-two.

IDEAL FURNITURE CO.

Date: 1908–1929
Location: then 516 West Fourth Street (Martyn Brothers Building)
Founders: Otto F. Lindholm, John Pearson, Sture F. Nelson and C.W. Nord
Products: pedestals and tabourets

Established and incorporated in 1908, the company held only $10,000 in capital stock. It was first located in the Martyn Brothers Building at then

Ideal Furniture Company. *Jamestown, New York, Historical and Industrial Review*, 1911.

516 West Fourth Street. M.W. Ward Company, Elite Furniture and Martyn Brothers were also located in that building.

In 1909, the operating officers of the company were Otto F. Lindholm, John Pearson, Sture F. Nelson and C.W. Nord. In 1911, entrepreneur Charles B. Coyle from New York City became the president of the company. Ideal may have been experiencing difficult times since its establishment, and Coyle had a reputation for successfully financing manufacturing projects. The vice-president was John Pearson, secretary was Otto F. Lindholm, treasurer was Sture F. Nelson and general manager and assistant treasurer was T.A. Morrow (a young man with a background in real estate). The company manufactured pedestals and tabourets in choice mahogany and native woods, marketing its products throughout the United States. In 1911, the company was listed at 61 Harrison Street, west across the river from Maddox Table. A flood in Brooklyn Square along the Chadakoin River occurred in 1911, which caused the company to relocate to Allen Street. Pearl City Furniture may have moved into the empty building on Harrison Street. The Allen Street building was a two-story structure with five thousand square feet of floor space. That building supplied steady work for fifteen skilled men.

In 1913, the fire department was called to the Ideal Furniture Company plant located on Allen Street. The fire originated in the second-floor finishing room and was probably due to spontaneous combustion of rags used in this room. The firemen responded quickly, saving the building from total destruction. No water was used in fighting the fire, which was extinguished quickly with chemicals. It was confined to the room, with damage caused entirely by fire and heat. The finishing room was badly damaged.

Ideal failed in 1929.

GLOBE CABINET CO.

Date: 1909–1916
Location: then 771 East Second Street
Founders: William Jones and Thure E. Linderholm
Products: countertops, veneered tables and desks

Globe Cabinet Company was established and incorporated in 1909. The company had two locations: 27 Taylor Street and 59 Harrison Street. Globe manufactured countertops, veneered tables and desks from

Globe Cabinet Company.
*Jamestown, New York,
Historical and Industrial
Review*, 1911.

mahogany and choice native woods. The countertops produced catered mostly to the metal furniture trade.

In 1911, Globe was in a two-story building made of sheet metal that formerly housed Co-Operative Cabinet, at then 27 Taylor Street. The structure had approximately eight thousand square feet of floor space. Its annual sales were upward of $30,000, with most of the revenue coming from the Jamestown area. In 1911, the operating officers were President William Jones and Secretary/Treasurer and General Manager Thure E. Linderholm. Globe moved again in 1913 or 1914 to a location on Blackstone Avenue. By 1916, Globe was out of business.

STANDARD TABLE CO.

Date: 1909–1927
Location: then 84–92 Steele Street
Founders: Charles S. Eddy and Leonard G. Cowing
Products: dining room tables

This company was established and incorporated in 1909. In 1911, Charles S. Eddy was president and Leonard G. Cowing was treasurer and manager. Cowing was previously secretary and general manager of Jamestown Veneer Door. The company was located in a three-story factory building at then 84–92 Steele Street. Banner Furniture had previously occupied that building. In 1911, Standard employed approximately forty skilled men in twelve thousand square feet of floor space. The company was equipped with the newest machinery and appliances. Standard produced dining room tables in quartered oak and other fine woods. Two traveling salesmen marketed the product throughout the United States. Standard failed in 1927. In 1928, Monitor Furniture occupied the Steele Street location.

ELITE FURNITURE CO.

Date: 1909–1953
Location: then 516 West Fourth Street (Martyn Brothers Building)

Founders: Gustaf D. Danielson, Charles J. Anderson, Gustaf A. Lawson,
   Robert E. Jones and Axel E. Bloomquist
Products: library and davenport table, pedestals and tabourets

The primary founders of Elite Furniture pooled their resources from the
time they were established, which made the company a success for over forty
years. Elite incorporated in March 1909, founded by Gustaf D. Danielson
and about thirteen investors. Charles J. Anderson, a shoe merchant in
Jamestown, became president, Danielson was named vice-president,
Gustaf A. Lawson was treasurer, Robert E. Jones was secretary and Axel E.
Bloomquist was the general manager of the newly formed company.

   Charles Anderson was born in Sweden in June 1862. He was educated
there and learned the shoemaking trade. He came to the United States and
settled in Jamestown at the age of eighteen in 1880. For two and a half years,
he repaired, made and sold shoes in his little shop. He went into partnership
with C.W. Gripp, another shoemaker in Jamestown. That first store was
located on East Second Street. After three years, they moved to a new
location, and Anderson purchased Gripp's interest. At one time, Anderson
owned as many as five shoe stores in the area and Pennsylvania. He became
somewhat of an entrepreneur, acquiring holdings in the Elite Furniture
Company, Jamestown Car Parts Company (a forerunner of Blackstone
Corporation) and Jamestown Metal Desk Company. He ran a steamboat
ticket agency in Jamestown, and one of the lines represented was the White
Star Line. Anderson died in December 1937 at the age of sixty-three.

   Axel E. Bloomquist was born in Sweden in 1871. He went to a private
school and learned the art and craft of designing and making furniture. He
was twenty when he came to Jamestown, finding work as a cabinetmaker. He
became president of Elite Furniture after the death of Anderson. Bloomquist
died in August 1962 at the age of ninety-one.

   Gustaf Danielson was born in Sweden in 1873. He came to the United
States in 1890 as a full-fledged cabinetmaker. He was only seventeen years
old but had no trouble finding jobs in the Jamestown furniture industry.
He first worked at Jamestown Chair Company and then at Maddox Table
Company. He joined a group of coworkers at Maddox Table who were
looking to pool their money for a business venture. They started a small
cabinet shop and named it Jamestown Co-Operative Cabinet. Located first
at 27 Taylor Street, it was listed in the city directory in 1905. By 1908, the
building housed Globe Cabinet. Danielson moved from that business and
became a founder and the vice-president of Elite Furniture.

Elite manufactured a better grade of library and davenport table, pedestals and tabourets. Until about 1914, it was located in the former Martyn Furniture Factory on 516 West Fourth Street. In 1915, Elite had moved into a new building at then 1076–86 Allen Street Extension next to the Atlas Furniture Co. The new building was a four-story frame structure, 54 by 112 feet, with a basement and elevators. Enough land was purchased at that time for the possibility of any expansion. The yard at the rear of the building had a private switch running from the Erie Railroad tracks to the loading and unloading docks. This dock allowed the company to buy larger amounts of raw material at better prices and ship larger volumes of finished goods to a larger distribution market. Each department foreman was made a stockholder, establishing an early precedent for employees sharing in a company's success. The company survived until 1953. Blackstone Corporation purchased the land and built a two-story complex at the location.

ELK FURNITURE CO.

Date: 1910–1933
Location: then 178–84 Blackstone Avenue
Founders: John A. Hallin, Frank A. Jacobson and Thure E. Linderholm
Products: library tables, pedestals and dining room furniture

Elk Furniture incorporated in 1910 but did not appear in the city directory until 1913. The president and general manager was John A. Hallin, vice-president was Frank A. Jacobson and secretary/treasurer was Thure E. Linderholm.

Elk specialized in library tables, pedestals and dining room furniture and was located in a two-story building with twenty thousand square feet of floor space at then 178–84 Blackstone Avenue. In 1920, the company employed thirty-five skilled workmen. It became Munson Furniture in 1933 for a short time. By 1943, Jamestown Metal Products occupied the building.

John Hallin was born in Smoland, Sweden, in 1874. After attending public school there, he decided to come to America. He arrived in Jamestown in 1892 and had little problem fitting in with the Swedish community. Many of the Swedish-speaking residents were from Smoland, and some even knew his family. His first job was at A.C. Norquist Company. He then went to Bailey,

Jones Company and finally to Liberty Furniture as a foreman for about seven years. In 1910, he and others formed the Elk Furniture Company, specializing in the manufacture of library tables and pedestals. Hallin died in November 1968 at the age of ninety-four.

JAMESTOWN CARVING AND MANUFACTURING CO.

Date: 1911–1915
Location: then 40–48 Steele Street
Founders: Vernie F. Anderson and Herbert F. Litch
Products: carvings for furniture, pianos and caskets

This company was founded in March 1911 with Vernie F. Anderson as president and Herbert F. Litch as secretary/treasurer. It manufactured fine carvings in mahogany and the choicest native woods for better grades of furniture, pianos and caskets. It was located at 40–48 Steele Street in a three-story concrete block structure with ten thousand square feet of floor space, the former site of Jamestown Art Carving Works. In 1913, the officers of the company were President E.N. Vanderwark, Vice-president and Secretary J.A. Peterson and Treasurer A.M. Vanderwark. The company survived until 1915.

PEARL CITY FURNITURE

Date: 1911–1920?
Location: then 59 Harrison Street
Founders: John and C.J. Lindbeck
Products: parlor and library tables, pedestals and tabourets

John Lindbeck and C.J. Lindbeck established this small shop in 1911. In 1915, the operating officers were President C.W. Eckman, Treasurer Lawrence Eckman, Secretary J.B. Eckman and Superintendent Carl E. Anderson. The shop produced parlor and library tables, pedestals and tabourets at the plant on Harrison Street. This building may have previously housed Ideal Furniture Company. In 1920, the building housed Acme Furniture. By 1932, Modern Cabinet Company was in the building.

PEERLESS FURNITURE CO.

Date: 1911–1913?
Location: then 12–16 River Street
Founders: Frank O. and Reynold Norquist
Products: bedroom furniture, buffets and china closets

Established and incorporated in 1911, the founders were Frank O. Norquist and his son Reynold. These two men were no strangers to the successful furniture industry in Jamestown. The Norquist name had been associated with fine furniture since 1881. The new building at then 12–16 River Street was on the site of the former Century Furniture Company. A large fire in 1910 destroyed the Century Building. The new factory was a large four-story structure eighty feet square, with over twenty-five thousand square feet of floor space. It was equipped with modern machinery and appliances. Its specialty was an inexpensive line of bedroom furniture, but higher-end buffet and china closets in mahogany and choice native woods were also produced by Peerless. In 1912, approximately thirty skilled workers were employed in various departments of the company.

By 1913, A.C. Norquist Company had taken over the interest of Peerless, and the city directory listed it as plant B of the Norquist Company.

JAMESTOWN UPHOLSTERY CO. (JAMESTOWN ROYAL UPHOLSTERY)

Date: 1913
Location: 300 Crescent Street
Founders: John H. Prather, Fred A. Nelson, Louis N. Olmsted and Frank Kling
Products: manufactured upholstered leather and fabric furniture

Established in 1913 as Jamestown Upholstery Company, the original officers were President John H. Prather, Vice-president Fred A. Nelson and Secretary/Treasurer Louis N. Olmsted. Frank Kling was the superintendent.

Fred A. Nelson was born in 1874, a native of Jamestown. His father was connected with the Jamestown Police Department and later in business with his son at Jamestown Upholstery. Fred attended the Jamestown public schools, graduating from Jamestown High School. While in school, he worked evenings at a Swedish bookstore. Nelson moved to his uncle's home in Rock Island, Illinois, after graduation. While there, he attended Augustana College, taking courses in business. He worked at a general store in the evenings and on Saturdays. He graduated in 1893 and returned to Jamestown to work for Jamestown Lounge Company as a clerk. He advanced and from 1900 to 1913 became a traveling salesman for the company. Showing a marked ability in sales, his territory grew to fourteen states. In 1913, Nelson had accumulated enough capital to become the prime mover in the organization of Jamestown Upholstery Company. The company manufactured fine upholstered furniture in leather and fabric and was located at 300 Crescent Street in Jamestown. The building was four stories high with twenty-four thousand square feet of floor space. In 1913, every device of a mechanical nature without depreciating quality that could be advantageously used was installed. Electric power was installed, and a 150-horsepower boiler was added in anticipation of expansion.

In 1916, three years after its establishment, Fred Nelson became president of the company. Prior to the founding of Jamestown Upholstery, he had worked at Jamestown Lounge Company for twenty years. Carl A. Hultquist was associated with him in the active management of the business. Nelson, Clarence A. Hultquist (a retail merchant in the city) and Secretary/Treasurer Earle O. Hultquist of Art Metal Construction Company constituted the board of directors. There were approximately twenty-five people employed when the company started. By 1920, the company had grown and employed about forty skilled office and management personnel.

During the First World War, the company manufactured fine leather cushions for U.S. Navy torpedo boat destroyers. Jamestown Royal also made all the furniture used by the Supreme Court justices, including Jamestown's own Robert H. Jackson. Through the years, Jamestown Royal was known for its high-quality furniture. Lucille Ball also purchased furniture from Jamestown Royal.

Around 1929, the name changed to Jamestown Royal Upholstery after buying Royal Upholstery, located at 16 Scott Street. The company is still in business today manufacturing made-to-order furniture.

JAMESTOWN FANCY FURNITURE CO.

Date: 1913–1921?
Location: then 17–19 Scott Street
Founders: Rudolph W. Schulze and Abe DeGoed
Products: pedestals, tabourets and smoking stands

Established in 1913 by Rudolph W. Schulze and Abe DeGoed, this company produced a fine line of pedestals, tabourets and smoking stands in a building located at then 17–19 Scott Street. Schulze built the two-story building, which was 60 by 110 feet. In 1915, a new addition was erected. By 1920, the company employed approximately thirty workmen. The company was gone in 1921. Royal Upholstery Company may have taken over the building.

Rudolph Schulze was born in February 1885. He was a woodcarver by trade, working in Michigan furniture factories. He became proficient in his trade and possessed a thorough understanding of most of the machines used in woodworking. He formed a partnership under the established name of Schulze and Van Stee, but it dissolved in 1913. Rudolph went on to establish Jamestown Fancy Furniture Company

MONARCH FURNITURE CO.

Date: 1915–1932
Location: then 712 East Second Street
Founders: Oscar E. Anderson and Marcus J. Norquist
Products: dining room furniture

Established in 1915, this company was founded by two well-known local furniture men, Oscar E. Anderson and Marcus J. Norquist, to build dining room furniture. Twenty-five artisans were initially employed. In 1917, the president of the company was Oscar Anderson; Frank O. Anderson, the brother of Oscar and successful owner of Empire Furniture, was vice-president; the secretary was Milton Schafer; and the treasurer was Alfred A. Anderson, another brother. Its fine dining room furniture was offered in many styles and colors to a broad customer base. During the early years, the business's success allowed it to move into the abandoned Munson and Johnson Building at then 712 East Second Street. The building burned in

Monarch Furniture billhead. *Courtesy of Fenton History Center.*

August 1924, but the company recovered. It did not succeed very far and was gone by 1932 or 1933. The building was taken over by Manufacturer's Outlet Co.

CADWELL-VERNON CO.

Date: 1915–1920
Location: then 115 Foote Avenue
Founders: John and Eugene Cadwell and Dixon S. and Frank S. Vernon
Products: wood and metal furniture

Founded in 1915, the company was formerly known as Cadwell Cabinet and was established in 1899 by John and Eugene Cadwell. The newly established company officers were John and Eugene Cadwell and Dixon S. and Frank S. Vernon. It produced both wood furniture and metal products. The location of the company was the same as the previous Cadwell Cabinet at then 115 Foote Avenue. By 1920, Penrod Walnut and Veneer Company occupied the building.

ACTIVE FURNITURE CO.

Date: 1916–1932?
Location: then 40–42 Steele Street

Founders: Nestor Munson, Oscar Newgren and O.R. Johnson
Products: phonograph cases and parlor and library tables

Established and incorporated in 1916, the officers were men who learned the furniture making trade by hands-on experience. Nestor Munson was elected president, Oscar Newgren was vice-president and O.R. Johnson was secretary/treasurer at the time of its inception. Twelve men were initially employed besides the founders. By 1920, the company's success allowed it to reach a workforce of thirty-five skilled employees. The company produced high-grade phonograph cases and parlor and library tables. The first plant was located at then 40–42 Steele Street.

In 1918, the company moved into the abandoned Window Screen Company plant located at 151 Jones and Gifford Avenue. Steam boilers powered this new location. The officers at that time were President Carl R. Carlson, First Vice-president Charles A. Johnson, Second Vice-president George Jacobson and Secretary/Treasurer and General Manager Oscar R. Bard. In 1920, the company officers were President Carl R. Carlson and Secretary/Treasurer Oscar Bard. The last year Active Furniture is listed in the city directory is 1932.

Oscar R. Bard was born in Smoland, Sweden, in January 1882. He attended school there and worked on his father's farm. He came to this country at the age of fourteen after gaining a good elementary education in Sweden. Upon his arrival in 1896, he moved in with a brother in Falconer, New York. For the first three months, Bard attended school so he might gain an insight into American ways. He then went to work for Jamestown Mantel Company in Falconer. He learned the trade of a cabinetmaker and remained there for ten years. He was given the opportunity to better himself by finding employment at the Bennett Piano Company in Warren, Pennsylvania. He remained there for two years before entering a partnership with his brother Charles S. Bard, making furniture and office fixtures. Some years later, he turned his interest to the retail shoe business, becoming a partner with Victor Johnson, the firm becoming Johnson & Bard located on Second Street. After about seven years, Oscar turned his attention to the monumental works of August Gustafson on North Main Street. He entered into a partnership under the firm name of Gustafson & Bard Monumental Works of Jamestown. Still connected with the Active Furniture Company, he became secretary/treasurer in 1918.

Carl R. Carlson was born in March 1885 in Smoland, Sweden. As a young lad, he worked on his father's farm and attended public school in Sweden.

When he became of age, he went to work in a door factory. Carlson worked there until he was twenty years old. Looking for greater opportunities, he came to Jamestown in 1905. Upon his arrival, he went to work for Anchor Furniture Company. He remained there for almost nine years, leaving for a better position at Superior Furniture Company, working on a band saw. Two years later, he joined the newly organized Active Furniture Company, and in 1918, he was elected president and superintendent of the company.

Advance Furniture Co.

Date: 1916–1950
Location: then 101–27 Hopkins Avenue
Founders: Joseph Carlson, Hjalmar Rosenquist and August A. Sandberg
Product: bedroom furniture

This was another of the many industries in Jamestown that sprung from the founders' common roots in Smoland, Sweden. Organized in 1916 and incorporated in April of that year, the founders and operating officers were President Joseph Carlson, Vice-president Hjalmar Rosenquist and Secretary/Treasurer August A. Sandberg, who also formed Alliance Furniture. A building was erected in April, and operations began in August. Eighteen men plus the founders of the company produced medium-grade bedroom furniture. By 1920, the company had almost doubled in size and included the most modern equipment for the production of furniture. As was common in those days, the company officers held other positions on the shop floor. Carlson was the superintendent, while Rosenquist supervised packing and shipping. August Sandberg held the position of office manager. Located at then 101–27 Hopkins Avenue, the company grew steadily until the workforce reached more than one hundred and the buildings spread over eighty thousand square feet. By 1950, the company was out of business, and the buildings became part of Hope's Windows complex.

Hjalmar Rosenquist was born in Smoland in 1883. At the age of fourteen, he apprenticed as a woodcarver. He came to the United States at the age of eighteen, settling in Jamestown's Swedish community. His father was already a resident of the city, having come from Sweden in 1901. During the day, Hjalmar worked at Norquist Brothers furniture factory and attended school at night. After two years, when the Norquist plant was gutted by fire,

Hjalmar Rosenquist. *History of Chautauqua County and Its People*, 1921.

he worked at Automatic Voting Machine for three months. He then went into woodworking at Union Furniture Company as a carver. Remaining with that company for one year, he took a position in the case-making department of Art Metal Construction Company. After a number of years at Metallic Furniture in Jamestown and Chicago, he and others formed Advance Furniture Company in 1916.

August Sandberg was born in Smoland in January 1878. He attended school there until the age of twelve, when his family came to this country and settled in Jamestown. He continued his education and worked at various minor occupations after school to help support the family. Eventually, he entered Atlas Furniture Company and later Alliance Furniture. While at Alliance, he became familiar with cabinetmaking and was a skilled woodcarver. He enrolled at Jamestown Business School and earned a business degree. August's father, Alfred, died in 1894 when August was only sixteen. August had to support himself, taking a position as clerk at H.P. Robertson Company. He quickly advanced to the executive offices, with greater responsibility for the business end of furniture manufacturing. In 1916, he and other investors founded Advance Furniture Company. August Sandberg died in 1951 at the age of seventy-two.

Joseph Carlson was born in Sweden in March 1880. He received a good education in the schools of Sweden and at the age of sixteen decided to learn the trade of a cabinetmaker. He worked at that trade in Sweden for approximately seven years. By the time he came to Jamestown in

Joseph Carlson. *History of Chautauqua County and Its People*, 1921.

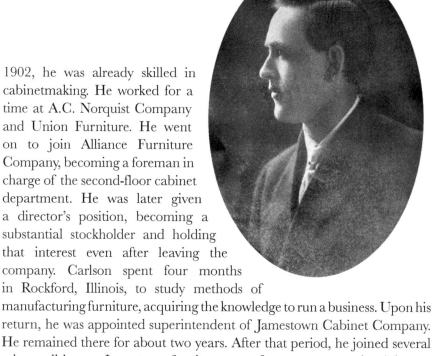

1902, he was already skilled in cabinetmaking. He worked for a time at A.C. Norquist Company and Union Furniture. He went on to join Alliance Furniture Company, becoming a foreman in charge of the second-floor cabinet department. He was later given a director's position, becoming a substantial stockholder and holding that interest even after leaving the company. Carlson spent four months in Rockford, Illinois, to study methods of manufacturing furniture, acquiring the knowledge to run a business. Upon his return, he was appointed superintendent of Jamestown Cabinet Company. He remained there for about two years. After that period, he joined several other well-known Jamestown furniture manufacturers to organize Advance Furniture Company. He died in 1962 at the age of eighty-two.

ACME FURNITURE CO.

Date: 1916–1930
Location: then 61 Harrison Street
Founder: Carl L. Liedblad
Products: library tables, tabourets and pedestals

Carl L. Liedblad established this company in 1916. He was also the president. The vice-president was J. Ernest Johnson and secretary was Carl S. Liedblad, son of the founder. Both father and son were brought up in the furniture industry and by trade were furniture finishers working with stains and varnishes. Acme manufactured library tables, tabourets and pedestals.

In 1920, the company employed thirty workers. It was located at then 61 Harrison Street, west of the Chadakoin River, in a building with 1,300 square feet of floor space and equipped with the most modern machinery of its kind. In 1928, Earle R. Morrison purchased the plant, equipment, stock and real property of the company on Harrison Street. Included in that sale was a 245- by 259-foot lot located on Blackstone Avenue. In 1932, Modern Cabinet Company occupied the building on Harrison Street.

Carl L. Liedblad was born in 1867. He began his education in Jamestown schools, leaving at age ten to work at the Broadhead Mills to help support his family. He finished his education by attending school part time. He left Broadhead Mills to work for the Breed Furniture Company. He spent four years learning the trade of a wood finisher. He left Breed Company for a short time to work for Beman, Breed & Phillips. He also worked for C.J. Norquist, Maddox, Bailey Company, Blanchard & Miller and C.W. Herrick Company.

Carl S. Liedblad was born in Jamestown in 1895, the son of Carl L. Liedblad. He was given every opportunity to gain a good business education. Upon graduation, he learned his father's trade, that of a furniture finisher. Carl went to work at C.W. Herrick Company in Falconer, a company his father helped to organize. He then went to Marvel Furniture and finally joined his father at Acme.

JAMESTOWN FURNITURE EXPOSITION BUILDING

The first furniture exposition was held in 1895 at the Celeron auditorium. The next one was not held until 1917, when the Exposition Building was completed in downtown Jamestown. The building was started in 1916 and completed the next year. A nine-story fireproof building with 186,000 square feet of floor space had the distinction of being the tallest structure in Jamestown, built at a cost equivalent today to $250,000. The first business manager was Louis J. Jagger, a well-known Jamestown furniture businessman. This semiannual show for as many as 1,500 retail buyers was traditionally held in January and June. Jamestown manufacturers broke that mold and started holding the shows in November and May. This enabled the buyers to plan for post-Christmas and Fourth of July peak periods. This innovation was extremely popular with out-of-town retail buyers and gave Jamestown a noteworthy distinction in the highly competitive furniture market. Another unique and popular activity was to host buyers in private homes throughout the Jamestown area. The warm hospitality and personal touch gave the Jamestown-area furniture industry the distinction of being in the "friendship business." As the show grew in popularity, the entire group of out-of-town buyers could not be accommodated in private homes. As a result, the Hotel Jamestown was built.

It did not take long for the competition to slow the momentum gained by the success of the furniture mart. The Grand Rapids, Michigan and Chicago markets responded fiercely and stepped up their marketing efforts. Southern firms were also developing a highly competitive case goods marketing center at High Point, North Carolina, and came on very strong in promoting their shows. Jamestown took on a different marketing strategy while keeping up with the changes to remain competitive.

Throughout the ensuing time, space limitations at the furniture mart prevented expansion of the show. Local companies were given priority over outside manufacturers, which led to the show taking on an increasingly regional character.

Finally, furniture manufacturing in Jamestown experienced a lack of growth and market share. The southern manufactories took over a big portion of the industry. It made good business sense to locate the show where the bulk of the furniture was being produced.

Allied Furniture Co.

Date: 1919–1929
Location: then 56 River Street (behind A.C. Norquist)
Founders: Frank O. Norquist, Austin E. Anderson and Reynold Norquist
Products: bedroom furniture

Responsible men of direction who had been in the busy center of Jamestown furniture manufacturing for many years established Allied Furniture in 1919. They were Frank O. Norquist and Austin E. Anderson, founders of Superior Furniture Company. The secretary/treasurer was Reynold Norquist, Frank's son.

This newly established company manufactured bedroom furniture and in 1922 located in a new plant at then 56 River Street. The plant was equipped with all the modern mechanical woodworking devices necessary for the expeditious production of bedroom furniture.

In 1920, the company employed approximately fifty workmen. By 1929, it was out of business. The building was still vacant in 1930, and sometime after that, it was taken over by A.C. Norquist Company and demolished.

MONITOR FURNITURE CO.

Date: 1919–1980
Location: first location West Fifth Street (Martyn Brothers Building)
Founder: Charles Gustafson
Products: phonograph cabinets and miscellaneous solid cherry furniture

Monitor desk. *Courtesy of Fenton History Center.*

Founder Charles Gustafson and forty-six furniture workers established Monitor in 1919. They pooled their money and skills to build solid cherry furniture and phonograph cabinets for the Edison Company. Its first location was in the old Martyn Furniture building on West Fifth Street, remaining there until about 1926. The officers and founders were President Andrew Nylander, Vice-president Oscar Nelson and Secretary/Treasurer Arvid Eckberg. The company's early development was strongly influenced by the leadership of John A. Peterson. He joined the company soon after it was founded, becoming vice-president. In 1922, the officers were President C.M. Alfred Peterson, Vice-president Charles B. Gustafson, Secretary Henry C. Halberg and Treasurer F. Albert Munson.

In the early 1920s, there was a sudden drop in the need of phonograph cabinets, attributed to the advent of the radio. Monitor shut down for a year, with its inventory of cabinets stacked high in the plant, while the directors searched for a new line of furniture. It began producing a top-end furniture line that included desks, secretaries and case goods (bedroom and dining room furniture).

In 1926, the company moved to a structure that had previously been part of Standard Table at then 92 Steele Street near the present power plant. Monitor was sold in 1980 to Provost, a French company. By 1983, the company was out of business.

PREMIER FURNITURE CO.

Date: 1920–1936
Located: then 61 Water Street
Founder: Marcus J. Norquist
Products: dining and bedroom furniture

This company was established in 1920 with Marcus J. Norquist as founder and president. Its location was then 61 Water Street in a two-story building that housed the former Eagle Furniture Company. The name changed to Premier Cabinet Corp. in 1921. Dining and bedroom furniture was built in five thousand square feet of floor space. The company was gone by 1936, and the building no longer exists.

STRATTON FURNITURE CO.

Date: 1920–1932?
Location: Steele Street (behind H.P. Robertson)
Founders: D.V. Stratton, J.B. Farwell, C.M. Kinnear and J.E. Sheedy
Products: tables and bedroom sets

Incorporated in 1920 with $250,000 of capital, this company took over the shop of Nelson & Company on Steele Street behind the H.P. Robertson furniture factory. The plant was converted over from manufacturing tables to building bedroom sets. The officers were President D.V. Stratton, Vice-president J.B. Farwell, Secretary C.M Kinnear and Treasurer J.E. Sheedy. There is no record of this company in the Jamestown City Directories. It was out of business by about 1932.

EPILOGUE

By the mid-1920s, small family-owned companies were feeling the burden of increased shipping costs and expense of modernization. By the late 1930s, the heyday of furniture manufacturing in Jamestown was waning. It marked the end of an era of phenomenal growth and prosperity for the industry and the city of Jamestown. One important factor contributing to the loss was the influence of the newly formed southern markets and abundant virgin forestland. Many southern plants began as sawmills, gradually extending operations to furniture production with great success. They gained a competitive edge by increasing productivity with cheaper labor, providing a quality product at a lower price. Those newly formed southern companies were run by very good businessmen who knew how to build and market their furniture in big metropolitan cities.

Another factor that attributed to the downturn of furniture manufacture in Jamestown was the plight of small family-owned businesses. Strict financial management taught by the Depression was not always available to these companies. Owners lacked the necessary capital to hire financial advisors. They also lacked the capital to expand facilities and purchase labor-saving machinery. With the advent of large department stores, retailers preferred to do business with larger companies offering a broad range of household furnishings.

Another reason for the decline was the increase in metal fabrication. This industry offered better wages due to a higher degree of mechanization. A single worker could run a number of machines, achieving higher productivity. On the other hand, woodworking required a more labor-intensive production method. This meant that the margin of sales had to be spread among more workers, resulting in lower wages.

The issue of labor and management differences in the early days was looked on as a one-way street. The development of organized labor was not considered progress. Perhaps owners and unions should have made more of an effort to work together. In those days, the activities of strong radical labor factions impacted many larger cities in the United States. This activity may have contributed to the strife of organizing labor in Jamestown.

Timeline of Furniture Shops, 1816–1930s

Keyes & Breed History

Start Date	Close	Name	Became	Specialized In	Location	Swedish Founders
1816	1821	Royal Keyes	Keyes & Breed	tables, stands & chairs	Main St.	
1821	1822	Keyes & Breed	Wm. & J.C. Breed	bureaus, bedsteads	Main St.	
1823	1852	Wm. & J.C. Breed	D.C. Breed Co.	dining, dressing & worktables	Pine St.	
1853	1866	D.C. Breed Co.	D.C. & J.W. Breed Co.	sideboards, secretaries	Winsor & Willard	
1867	1880	D.C. & J.W. Breed Co.	D.C. Breed Co.	same as all above	105 Winsor	
1881	1893	D.C. Breed Co.	Breed-Johnson Co.	same as all above	105 Winsor	
1894	1912	Breed-Johnson Co.	Eckman Furniture	same as all above	Jones & Gifford	S

TIMELINE OF OTHERS

START DATE	CLOSE	NAME	BECAME	SPECIALIZED IN	LOCATION	SWEDISH FOUNDERS
1827	1829	Palmiter Chair Factory	R.V. Cunningham	flag & wood seat chairs	1st St.	
1829	1860	R.V. Cunningham		flag & wood seat chairs	3rd & Cherry	
1838	1846	Marsh, Bell & Robinson	Rogers & Bell	cane & flag seat chairs	Winsor & Willard	
1839	1846	Benham & Bell	may have become Rogers & Bell	Boston rockers	Winsor & Willard	
1846	1851	Rogers & Bell	Flint & Warner	chairs in knockdown version	Winsor & Willard	
1851	1854	Flint & Warner	Flint, Hall & Moses	chairs in knockdown version	Winsor & Willard	
1852	1854	Sampson & Tyrrel Co.	Simmons & Tyrrel Co.	variety of chairs & bedsteads	Main St.	
1854	1860	Simmons & Tyrrel Co.	F. Simmons Co.	variety of chairs & bedsteads	Main St.	
1850s	1871	Ford, Wood & Co.	Wood & Co.	chairs & general line of furniture	Main St.	
1854	1855	Flint, Hall & Moses	Parks Bros.	chairs in knock-down version	Winsor & Willard	
1860	1864	F. Simmons & Co.		general line of furniture	105 Winsor	
1865	1920	Martyn Bros.		lounges	4th & 5th St.	
1867	1876	Joseph J. Gates Co.		cane-seat chairs	24 Main St.	
1868	1896	O.G. Chase & Son		wood-seat chairs	24 Main St.	

Start Date	Close	Name	Became	Specialized In	Location	Swedish Founders
1869	1876	Parks Brothers		general line of furniture	Main St.	
1869	1915	Lindblad Brothers Furniture		general line of furniture & veneer doors	11 Harrison St.	S
1870	1899	Jamestown Cane-Seat Chair Co.		cane, perforated, flag chairs & fancy rockers	Taylor St.	
1871	1880	Wood & Co.	for a short time was Wood & Comstock	general line of furniture	Main St.	
1872	1890s	Schildmacher & Bauer Co.		kitchen furniture & chairs	Main St.	
1873	1892	Jamestown Wood Seat Chair Co.		chairs	22 Steele St.	
1873	1904	Jamestown Bedstead Co.	H.P. Robertson Co.	bedsteads, cribs & tables	22 Steele St.	
1874	1903	A.P. Olson Co.	Diamond Furniture	tables	Taylor St.	S
1875	1883	George B. Ford Co.	Ford & Hodgkins	tables	7 Forest Ave.	
1875	1889	J.R. Newman	H.J. Newman	beds	Brooklyn Square	
1877	1881	Splint Seat Chair Co.	Marsh & Firman	chairs	42 Winsor St.	
1878	1887	Perforated Chair Seat Co.		chairs	40 Winsor St.	
1878	1898	S.A. Carlson & Son		chamber sets	6–10 Willard St.	S
1878	1886	Landon & Co.	Himebaugh	bedsteads	Main St.	

TIMELINE OF FURNITURE SHOPS, 1816–1930s

START DATE	CLOSE	NAME	BECAME	SPECIALIZED IN	LOCATION	SWEDISH FOUNDERS
1880	1906	Y.W. Burtch & Co.	Jamestown Chair Co.	fine variety of chairs	20 Winsor St.	
1880	1962	Shearman Brothers Co.		lounges, couches & sofa beds	Shearman Place	
1881	1886	Marsh & Firman		splint seat chairs	42 Winsor St.	S
1881	1965	A.C. Norquist Co.		bedroom furniture	415–21 Chandler St.	
1883	1888	Ford & Hodgkins Co.	Hodgkins & Cadwell	tables	7 Forest Ave.	
1883	1887	Swedish Furniture MFG Co.	Atlas Furniture	bedroom furniture	301 Harrison St.	S
1885	1886	Phillips, Maddox & Co.	Morgan, Maddox	parlor tables	22 Steele St.	
1886	1894	C.E. Weeks & Co.		chamber sets & extension tables	Brooklyn Square	
1886	1928	Himebaugh Brothers.		dining room furniture, beds & cribs	14 Steele St. & Hallock St.	
1886	1891	Morgan, Maddox & Co.	Maddox & Bailey	parlor & library tables	560 E. 2nd St.	
1887	1941	Atlas Furniture	Crawford Furniture	bedroom furniture	Allen St. Ext.	S
1888	1984	Jamestown Lounge Co.		living room & library furniture	38–58 Winsor St.	

175

START DATE	CLOSE	NAME	BECAME	SPECIALIZED IN	LOCATION	SWEDISH FOUNDERS
1888	1890	O'Connell & Quigley	J.F. O'Connell & Co.	tables	Washington & 4th St.	
1888	1901	Hodgkins & Cadwell	Cadwell Cabinet Co.	tables	7 Forest Ave.	
1889	1895	H.J. Newman & Co.	Newman Manufacturing Co.	cribs & cots	7 Forest Ave.	
1890	?	Chautauqua Upholstery Co.		parlor suites, chairs & rockers	108–10 E. 3rd St.	
1890	1895	J.F. O'Connell & Co.		hall furniture, parlor & library tables	Jones & Gifford Ave.	
1890	?	Chautauqua Table & Cabinet Co.		tables	700 E. 2nd St.	S
1890	1894	Johnston, Lawson & Co.	Crescent Table	parlor & library tables	118 Foote Ave.	S
1890	1906	Morgan MFG. Co.	Jamestown Table	tables	145–53 Fairmount Ave.	
1890	1903	Jamestown Desk Co.		roller door bookcases	20–26 Steele St.	
1890	1898	Maddox, Bailey & Co.	Bailey, Jones	tables	560 E. 2nd St.	
1891	1899	Chautauqua Furniture Co.		tables & desks	2nd St.	
1892	1890s	Benson, Hand & Frisbee		parlor tables	10–22 Steele St.	

Start Date	Close	Name	Became	Specialized In	Location	Swedish Founders
1894	1898	Crescent Table Co.		parlor & library tables	118 Foote Ave.	
1894	1953	Empire Furniture Co.		chamber suites & bedroom furniture	142 Foote Ave.	S
1895	1899	Newman Manufacturing Co.		cribs & cots	Holmes St.	
1895	1903	Munson & Waite Co.	Munson & Johnson	wood mantels	710–12 E. 2nd & Winsor St.	
1895	1903	Jamestown Veneer Works	Pearl City Veneer	veneer strips & misc. furniture	18–20 Steele St.	
1895	1906	Jamestown Furniture Co.	part of F.M. Curtis Co.	parlor tables & desks	West Main St.	
1898	1904	Bailey, Jones Co.	Bailey Table	parlor & library tables	105 Winsor St.	
1898	1984	Maddox Table Co.		parlor, library & office tables	101–25 Harrison St.	
1899	1915	Cadwell Cabinet Co.	Cadwell, Vernon Co.	office and bank furniture	123 Foote Ave.	
1899	1939	Star Furniture Co.		bookcases, dressers, bedroom furniture	40–44 Steele St.	
1900	1914	Ward Cabinet Co.		office and store fixtures	518 W. 4th St.	
1900	1910	Finley MFG Co.		kitchen tables & ironing boards	50 Steele St.	
1901	1946	Broden Table		library tables	714 W. 2nd St.	S

Start Date	Close	Name	Became	Specialized In	Location	Swedish Founders
1901	1994	Union Furniture	Union National	buffets, china cabinets, dining room furniture	226 Crescent St.	S
1902	1910	Century Furniture Co.	Peerless Furniture Co.	buffets, china cabinets	12–16 River St.	S
1902	1941	Anchor Furniture Co.		folding desks, parlor & library tables	8–20 Holmes St.	S
1902	1936	Diamond Furniture Co.		tables	46 Taylor St.	S
1902	1905	Anderson Veneer Door Co.	Jamestown Veneer Door	doors & misc. furniture	111–19 Cheney St.	S
1902	1922	F.M. Curtis Co.	Merriman Furniture Co.	bedroom furniture	716–18 E. 2nd St.	
1902	1993	Jamestown Panel & Veneer Co.	Jamestown Veneer & Plywood Co.	veneer strips & misc. furniture	50 Steele St.	
1902	1949	Seaburg MFG. Co.		phonograph cabinets, library tables	124–30 Steele St.	S
1903	1922	Nelson & Co.	Stratton Furniture	dining tables	40–48 Steele St.	S
1903	1914	Munson & Johnson Co.		wood mantels	710–12 E. 2nd & Winsor St.	S
1903	1924	Pearl City Veneer		veneer strips, dining & bedroom furniture	40–42 Steele St.	

Timeline of Furniture Shops, 1816–1930s

Start Date	Close	Name	Became	Specialized In	Location	Swedish Founders
1903	1909	Liberty Furniture Co.	part of Atlas Furniture	dressers, chiffoniers & dressing tables	11–15 Blackstone Ave.	S
1904	1929	Level Furniture Co.		library & parlor tables, phonograph cabinets	Allen St. Ext.	S
1904	1912	Golden Furniture Co.		dressers, chiffoniers	516 W. 4th St.	S
1904	1932	Marvel Furniture Co.		bedroom furniture, chiffoniers, dressers	1077 Allen St.	S
1904	1930	Bailey Table Co.		parlor & library tables, dining room suites	105 Winsor St.	
1905	1910	Jamestown Veneer Co.		veneer doors & tables	50 Steele St.	S
1905	1931	H.P. Robertson Co.	Tillotson Furniture	tables & folding beds	22 Steele St.	S
1905	1952	Alliance Furniture Co.	part of Tillotson Furniture	dining room furniture	611–15 Allen St.	S
1905	1940	National Furniture	Union National	parlor & library tables, bedroom sets	150 Blackstone Ave.	S
1905	1927	Eckman Furniture Co.	part of Randolph Furniture Works	desks, dining room & bedroom furniture	129 Jones & Gifford Ave.	S
1906	1965	Jamestown Table Co.	Taylor Jamestown	parlor & library tables	145–53 Fairmount Ave.	

Timeline of Furniture Shops, 1816–1930s

Start Date	Close	Name	Became	Specialized in	Location	Swedish Founders
1906	1932	Jamestown Chair Co.		rocker & dining room chairs	20 Winsor St.	S
1907	1933	American Carving Works	Van Stee Corp.	woodcarvings, folding tables & misc. furniture	516 W. 4th St.	
1907	1920	Eagle Furniture Co.	Premier Cabinet Co.	pedestals & tabourets	61 Water St.	S
1907	1913	Chadakoin Furniture Co.	Jamestown Carving & MFG	parlor & library tables	100 Steele St.	
1908	1920	Jamestown Cabinet Co.		phonograph cabinets, chiffoniers, misc. furniture	771 E. 2nd St.	
1908	1938	Superior Furniture Co.		dining & extension tables	167 Jones & Gifford Ave.	S
1908	1929	Ideal Furniture		pedestals & tabourets	516 W. 4th St.	S
1909	1916	Globe Cabinet Co.		desks & misc. furniture	27 Taylor St.	
1909	1927	Standard Table Co.	part of Monitor Furniture	dining room tables	84–92 Steele St.	
1909	1952	Elite Furniture Co.		library & davenport tables	516 W. 4th St.	S
1910	1933	Elk Furniture Co.	Munson Furniture	library tables, pedestals & dining room suites	178–84 Blackstone Ave.	
1911	1915	Jamestown Carving & MFG Co.		piano cabinets & caskets	40–48 Steele St.	
1911	1920	Pearl City Furniture		parlor & library tables, pedestals & tabourets	59 Harrison St.	

Start Date	Close	Name	Became	Specialized In	Location	Swedish Founders
1911	1913	Peerless Furniture Co.	part of A.C. Norquist	bedroom furniture, buffets & china cabinets	12–16 River St.	
1913	1929	Jamestown Upholstery Co.	Jamestown Royal Upholstery	leather & upholstered furniture	300 Crescent St.	S
1913	1921	Jamestown Fancy Furniture Co.		pedestals & furniture ornaments	17–19 Scott St.	
1915	1933	Monarch Furniture Co.		dining room furniture	712 E. 2nd St.	S
1915	1920	Cadwell-Vernon Co.		wood & metal furniture	115 Foote Ave.	S
1916	1932	Active Furniture Co.		phonograph cases, parlor & library tables	40–42 Steele St.	S
1916	1950	Advance Furniture Co.		bedroom furniture	101–27 Hopkins Ave.	S
1916	1928	Acme Furniture Co.	part of Modern Cabinet Co.	library tables, tabourets & pedestals	61 Harrison St.	S
1919	1929	Allied Furniture Co.		bedroom furniture	56 River St.	S
1920	1981	Monitor Furniture Co.	Eaton-Provost, Ltd.	phonograph cabinets, dining room furniture	92 Steele St.	S
1920	1922	Premier Furniture Co.	Premier Cabinet Corp.	bedroom furniture	61 Water St.	S
		Paterniti Table Co.			213 Hopkins Ave.	

START DATE	CLOSE	NAME	BECAME	SPECIALIZED IN	LOCATION	SWEDISH FOUNDERS
1920	1932?	**Stratton Furniture Co.**	Tillison Furniture	bedroom furniture	40–48 Steele St.	
1922	1938	**Premier Cabinet Corp.**	Plant II Maddox Table		61 Water St.	
1922	1926	**Merriman Furniture Co.**	Davis Furniture Co.	bedroom furniture	111–19 Cheney St.	

Bibliography

Anderson, A.W. *The Conquest of Chautauqua.* With excerpts from Hazeltine's 1877 book and notes by Foote. Jamestown, NY: Journal Press, Inc., 1932.

Child, Hamilton. *Chautauqua County Directory, 1873–1874.*

Civic & Industrial Progress of the Swedish People of Jamestown, 1848–1914. Jamestown, NY: Vartland Co., 1914.

Cook, George H., ed. *Industrial Advantages of Jamestown, N.Y.* N.p., 1890.

DeVillars, John J. *The Wood Furniture Mfg. Industry.* New Brunswick, NJ, 1949.

Dilley, Butler F., ed. *Biographical and Portrait Cyclopedia of Chautauqua County, New York.* Philadelphia: John M. Gresham & Co., 1891.

Doty, William J., ed. *The Historic Annals of Southwestern New York.* Vols. 1 and 2. New York: Lewis Historical Publishing Co. Inc., 1940.

Duliba, Leo E. *A Transition in Red: A History of the Jamestown, N.Y. Fire Department.* Merrick, NY: Richwood Publishing Co., 1976.

The Furniture Index. April 1915 and January 1920.

Hadley, Fenwick Y., and John P. Downs. *History of Chautauqua County and Its People*. Vols. 2 and 3. Boston: American Historical Society, Inc., 1921.

Hatch, Vernelle A. *Centennial History of Chautauqua County*. Vol. 3. Jamestown, NY: Chautauqua History Co., 1904.

———. *Illustrated History of Jamestown*. Jamestown, NY: C.E. Burk, 1900.

Jamestown City Directories, 1875–1940.

Jamestown Daily Journal, 1847–1881.

Jamestown Evening Journal, 1884–1931.

Jamestown, N.Y. Historical and Industrial Review. Issued by the Municipal Publishing Co., 1911.

Jamestown Post-Journal, 1950–1970.

Leet, Ernest D., ed. *History of Chautauqua County, New York, 1938–1978*. Westfield, NY: Chautauqua County Historical Society, 1980.

McMahon, Helen Grace. *Chautauqua County: A History*. N.p., 1958.

Merrill, Georgia Drew, and Obed Edson, eds. *History of Chautauqua County*. Boston: W.A. Fergusson & Co., 1894.

Moe, M. Lorimer, ed. *Saga from the Hills: A History of the Swedes of Jamestown*. N.p.: Fenton Historical Society, 1983.

Taylor, Ralph W. *Development of the Furniture Industry in Jamestown*. N.p., 1945.

Young, Andrew. *History of Chautauqua County, N.Y.* Buffalo, NY: Matthews & Warren, 1875. Reprint, Evansville, IN: Unigraph Inc., 1974.

Index

About the Author

Clarence Carlson is a Jamestown historian involved with the Fenton History Center as a board member and volunteer helping with guided historical tours of Jamestown and Lakeview Cemetery. He is a member of the Jamestown Historical Marker Committee. He is a retired purchasing buyer and expeditor with a number of Jamestown manufacturing companies.

Printed in the USA
CPSIA information can be obtained
at www.ICGtesting.com
LVHW071341210823
755779LV00039B/1266